*THE*

# CLUMSIEST
# PEOPLE
*IN*
# EUROPE.

FAVELL LEE MORTIMER

# THE
# CLUMSIEST
# PEOPLE
## IN
# EUROPE,

OR:

M^RS. MORTIMER'S BAD-TEMPERED GUIDE
TO THE VICTORIAN WORLD;

BY

## TODD PRUZAN

AND

## MRS. FAVELL LEE MORTIMER

(DECEASED).

BLOOMSBURY

# CONTENTS

———•———

## A BRIEF INTRODUCTION,

———•———

### PART I,

## THE CLUMSIEST PEOPLE IN EUROPE;

### SELECTIONS FROM
*The Countries of Europe Described,* 1849.

———————

# CONTENTS.

# CONTENTS.

— • —

## PART II,

# THE DRUNKEST LABOURERS IN ASIA;

### SELECTIONS FROM
*Far Off: Asia and Australia Described,* 1852.

# CONTENTS.

————•————

PART III,

# THE WICKEDEST CITY IN THE WORLD;

SELECTIONS FROM

*Far Off, Part II: Africa and America Described,* 1854.

# CONTENTS.

# INTRODUCTION.

———•••———

*IT'S 1855.* Do you know where your great-great-great-great-grandparents are? And more to the point: What's their problem?

No matter where your ancestors had the misfortune of living—no doubt smoking too much, or taking snuff, or reading useless novels—Mrs. Favell Lee Mortimer had something nasty to say about them. Their issues, according to Mrs. Mortimer, might have amounted to just about anything. The Irish "are very kind and good-natured when pleased, but if affronted, are filled with rage." In Italy, "the people are ignorant and wicked." In southern Sweden, "the cottages are uncomfortable."

Things were far, far worse in Asia and Africa. Take China, where "it is a common thing to stumble over the bodies of dead babies in the streets." Or Hindostan, where the women spend most of their time "in idleness, sauntering about and chattering nonsense." Or Abyssinia, where "one mother, who loved her children very much, punished her little girl for stealing honey, by burning the skin off her hands and lips."

For the better part of the nineteenth century, Mrs. Mortimer was something of a literary superstar to an impressionable audience, both in her native England and beyond. She published about a dozen children's books, and by the end of the century, her first and most popular title, *The Peep of Day*, had sold at least a million copies in thirty-eight languages, including Yoruba, Malayalim, Marathi-Balbodh, Tamil, Cree-Ojibbeway and French. In the middle of her forty-year career, Mrs. Mortimer published a geography trilogy: *The Countries of Europe Described* (1849), *Far Off, Part I: Asia and Australia Described* (1852), and *Far Off, Part II: Africa and America Described* (1854). Given her success at the time, it's not impossible that your own elders were schooled in Mrs. Mortimer's pronouncements on the world's many filthy, wicked, heathen cultures.

I found Mrs. Mortimer in an old barn. That's an odd place to waste a glorious August afternoon, but whenever I visit Martha's Vineyard, I can't resist spending a couple of hours in the barn that's now the Book Den East, with its attic full of swirling dust motes and faded magazines, farmers' almanacs and sheet music. It's still a mystery why, on my way toward the rickety wooden staircase one day, I noticed a small guidebook with a faded green spine perched halfway up the History shelf. The book's title, *The Countries of Europe Described*, certainly didn't grab my attention. Something so straightforward, so bland, with no author's name on the cover, must've been an ancient pocket encyclopedia, I figured.

When I pulled the book down, only vaguely curious, it fell open to a field guide to the habits of German women.

The ladies are very industrious, and wherever they go, they take their knitting. They are as fond of their knitting-needles as the gentlemen are of their pipes. The number of stockings they make would surprise you. How much better to knit than to smoke! When they are at home, the ladies spend a great deal of time in cooking; they also spin, and have a great deal of linen of their own spinning, locked up in great chests. Can they do nothing but knit, and cook, and spin? Yes, they can play on the piano, and the harp, and sing very sweetly. But they are not fond of reading useful books. When they read, it is novels about people who have never lived. It would be better to read nothing than such books.

The passage's escalating scorn and rudeness actually startled me, with its absolutist damnation of silly women and smoking and novels, certified by a publisher's commitment to type and paper and an ornate clothbound cover. Half an hour later, my friends and I sat around our backyard, drinking beer and passing the book around, hooting and slapping our wooden picnic table as we read aloud from the little book's casual condemnations of the Portuguese ("indolent, like the Spaniards"), the Jews ("very dirty"), the Icelanders ("I think it would almost make you sick to go to church in Iceland").

Yet months later, as I reread the book, I began to feel unsettled by its vicious, systematic country-by-country savaging of the entire world. I'd previously managed to get cheap laughs by reciting passages to dozens of people, and the cruel pronouncements inspired plenty of gleeful jeering. But now, it became impossible for me to spend even an hour in the book's stern company without feeling a little queasy.

That was partly because I found the writing style so engaging. The voice was direct, persuasive, forceful. The book relied on a no-

nonsense narrative tense we might term the second-person presumptuous (on the author's native England: "What country do you love best? Your *own* country. I know you do. Every child loves his own country best") and a healthy dose of enthralling *you-are-there* narration ("If you do not like Lisbon when you walk in it, you like it worse when you live there, because it is full of stinging insects; at night the musquitoes annoy you every moment"). The written word proved an efficient medium for documenting the faults of all ethnicities—from the Aborigines in Australia ("generally very harmless, unless provoked by ill-treatment") to the Zoolus in South Africa ("a miserable race of people"). Not to mention ignorant savages. And Buddhists. And Catholics.

Who would write such bad-tempered stuff? The title page of my 1852 edition of *The Countries of Europe Described* bore only the coy attribution "By the Author of 'The Peep of Day,' &c. &c." Casting my net into Google, I eventually came up with the name Favell Lee Mortimer, a Victorian children's writer known, if at all, for her first book, published in 1833: *The Peep of Day; or, a Series of the Earliest Religious Instruction the Infant Mind is Capable of Receiving.* Mrs. Mortimer was thirty-one when she published *Peep*, a Bible primer aimed at four-year-olds that now seems bizarrely and characteristically sadistic. Here's a glimpse at *Peep*'s terrifying opening chapter:

> God has covered your bones with flesh. Your flesh is soft and warm.
>
> In your flesh there is blood. God has put skin outside, and it covers your flesh and blood like a coat. . . . How kind of God it was to give you a body! I hope that your body will not get hurt. . . . Will your bones break?—Yes, they would, if you were to fall down from a high place, or if a cart were to go over them. . . .

How easy it would be to hurt your poor little body!

If it were to fall into the fire, it would be burned up. If a great knife were run through your body, the blood would come out. If a great box were to fall on your head, your head would be crushed. If you were to fall out of the window, your neck would be broken. If you were not to eat some food for a few days, your little body would be very sick, your breath would stop, and you would grow cold, and you would soon be dead.

Among Mrs. Mortimer's other enduring legacies was the innovative *Reading Disentangled* from 1834, a set of illustrated phonics cards that's been credited as the first flashcards in history. And her 1857 *Reading Without Tears* foreshadowed a meme of twentieth-century how-to book titles (*Divorce Without Tears*, *Sanskrit Without Tears*, *Sex Without Tears*) that's still in heavy rotation on Amazon.com. *Reading Without Tears* was ornately illustrated, and maybe a little loopy: "E is like a carriage with a little seat for the driver. F is like a tree with a seat for a child. G is like a monkey eating a cake . . ." Citing the book as a foundation of his early schooling, Sir Winston Churchill's memoir sniffed: "It certainly did not justify its title in my case."

BORN IN 1802 in Russell Square, London, Favell Lee Bevan was the daughter of David Bevan, a co-founder of Barclay, Bevan & Co., the bank now known as Barclays. Although she was raised a Quaker, at twenty-five Favell began exploring the Bible with a young family friend, Henry Manning. Their talks led them to a romantic tension that escalated with her conversion to Evangelicalism and his appointment to the clergy. By the time she was thirty, Favell's mother forbade her from writing to young Manning, and the triumph of Favell's 1833 publishing début, *The Peep of Day*, was trampled months later by Manning's marriage to a rector's daughter.

In 1841, at thirty-nine, Favell married the Rev. Thomas Mortimer—by most accounts a cruel, violent husband—and she spent much of her marriage at her brother's house, hiding out from her husband's rage. In 1847, Manning, whose wife had died after only four years of marriage, and who later became a cardinal, broke years of silence with Mrs. Mortimer by writing to her and asking her to return all the old letters he'd written to her. When Mrs. Mortimer asked him to reciprocate, he declined.

While Mrs. Mortimer was writing *The Countries of Europe Described*, the world was enduring unprecedented turbulence. In 1848, the fires of revolution raged through France, Austria, Switzerland, Italy, and more distant flashpoints from South Africa to Ceylon to Mexico. Yet any child reading *The Countries of Europe Described* in 1849 would have had no understanding that much of the world was in flames. "Superficial, incomplete, trifling! Such is the true character of this book," warned *Countries of Europe*'s pre-emptive introduction. "*Inaccurate* we hope it is not; but errors, in spite of care, may have crept in; and the world, old as she is, would not sit still for her picture."

At home in Broseley, Shropshire, just east of Wales, Mrs. Mortimer was suffering through tumult of her own: first, the death of her husband in November 1850, followed by even greater tragedy months later. Mrs. Mortimer's 1901 biography (called, perhaps inevitably, *The Author of The Peep of Day: Being the Life Story of Mrs Mortimer, by Her Niece Mrs Meyer*) describes her 1851 horror: "Mrs Mortimer, this spring, had the grief of hearing that her friend Henry Manning had become a Roman Catholic." It's difficult to read the anti-Catholic venom of Mrs. Mortimer's geography books without sensing the freshness of her romantic wounds. Ultimately, her great unrequited crush would ascend in the ranks of the Church; upon his death in 1892, Cardinal Manning was revealed to have regarded Mrs. Mortimer not as his first love but as his "spiritual mother." (No hard feelings.)

The 209 dully impassive pages of Mrs. Meyer's biography offer two striking revelations about Mrs. Mortimer's melancholy life. One is that, despite having written three authoritative geography books, full of omniscient, anthropological narratives that race from the Abyssinians to the Brazilians to the Dutch to the Zoolus, Mrs. Mortimer set foot outside England only twice in her life. As a teenager, she visited Brussels and Paris with her family; as a widow, after publishing her geographic trilogy, she made it as far as Edinburgh. Apart from that: nothing. Her sources were not her own experiences in foreign lands but hundreds of books, some of them decades old. Slogging through them surely wasn't an easy task, but shoe leather might have proved a useful research tool. Perhaps she could be forgiven for skipping out on Hindostan and Siberia—but Wales? Her writing desk in Broseley was just a few miles from the border.

The other revelation is that Mrs. Mortimer's personal life could be boiled down to an index of Victorian misery and misfortune, which her niece Mrs. Meyer cataloged with vicious delight. After just a few chapters, the lives of Mrs. Mortimer's family and friends devolve into a laundry list of spasmodic cholera, a face crushed by a wagon, erysipelas in the shins, the tail of a dressing gown set alight in a fireplace, influenza, water on the brain, an apoplectic fit, asthma, scarlatina, jaundice and pleurisy, blindness and deafness, bronchitis, and cerebral weakness. Mrs. Mortimer herself expired—over the course of eleven pages—in August 1878, at seventy-six.

In 1933, to mark the centennial of *The Peep of Day*, the *Times* of London published a caustic reminiscence of Mrs. Mortimer by her nephew, Edwyn Bevan, who acknowledged, "As a whole her life can hardly be thought to have been a happy one." Mrs. Meyer's 1901 biography put it less delicately: "Her doctor said she was the only person he ever met who wished to die."

*BUT WHAT HAPPENED* to Mrs. Mortimer's literary reputation? What happened to *The Countries of Europe Described*, to *Far Off Parts I* and *II*, to *Reading Without Tears*, to *Reading Disentangled*, to eleven other books? Actually, two are still in print. Paperback editions of *The Peep of Day* and its 1837 sequel, *Line Upon Line*, got a minor facelift in the 1890s, and their still-ominous updates are published today by Scotland's Christian Focus Publishing. Catherine MacKenzie, the publisher's children's editor, told me she knew little about Mrs. Mortimer, but she admitted that *Peep* and *Line*, while still biblically accurate, do give her the occasional chuckle.

Since the early 1700s, most writers of moral tracts for children offered comforting, compassionate fables and hymns to help the medicine go down. These writers, many of them women, fell into two camps: Rational Moralists taught practical lessons about living in the temporal world, while Sunday School Moralists, like Mrs. Mortimer, promised happiness and salvation through complete subservience to God. Meena Khorana, a professor of English and adolescent literature at Morgan State University in Baltimore, compared Mrs. Mortimer unfavorably to gentler predecessors like an eighteenth-century writer named Mary Sherwood. "She was very extreme, very didactic," Khorana said of Mrs. Mortimer. "She was not artistic compared to Mrs. Sherwood, who at least had narrative style and descriptions. Mrs. Mortimer's writing was more like spoken commands to children, basically trying to frighten them."

Eighteenth- and nineteenth-century Evangelicalists in Britain attacked social ills like drunkenness and gambling; perhaps the apex of their work was in influencing Britain's decision to abolish slavery throughout the Empire in 1833, the year *The Peep of Day* was published. Still, the Evangelicalists' educational and activist efforts don't seem entirely heartwarming today. Mrs. Mortimer's geography books leave us feeling morally dizzy, as one page grieves over slavery while the next ridicules the bloodthirsty As-Han-Tee warrior, the savage Dahomey worshipper, the stupid Bantu tribesman.

Obviously, writing as impolitic as Mrs. Mortimer's could not age particularly well, but her obscurity today is startling in the face of her innovative style and her brisk sales. Mrs. Mortimer vigilantly revised her three geography books for later editions, and updates stayed in print for decades after her death. But they also betray a startling, fascinating divergence from the evolving world map: she devotes sixty pages to Madagascar, fourteen pages to Greenland, and six sentences to New York City. And her books' geographic sequencing is downright jazzy. Lord knows why she decided to sandwich her chapter on Sicily between those on Iceland and Sweden.

Nevertheless, since they went out of print in the early twentieth century, the books and her name have nearly vanished from history. The most recent article about Mrs. Mortimer, a wry appreciation in the *New Yorker*, by her grandniece, Rosalind Constable, ran in 1950. Professors I contacted at the University of East Anglia proclaimed cluelessness, although they teach just twenty-four miles south of West Runton, Norfolk, a village perched atop a cliff above the North Sea, where Mrs. Mortimer spent her last sixteen years. The town historian of Sheringham, two miles away, told me he hadn't heard of her either. These days, Mrs. Mortimer even escapes the notice of the rare-book dealers who sell her works. When I purchased an 1854 Mortimer at the stately Manhattan shop Argosy Books, the proprietor asked me if I had an interest in witchcraft.

Yet contrary to what might seem obvious now, the greatest flaw in

Mrs. Mortimer's legacy wasn't so much her viciousness as her timing. Just as she picked up her pen, the Evangelicalists' belief system in Britain was reeling into a slow decline, and the country was enmeshed in industrial growing pains. In 1829, to Mrs. Mortimer's likely horror, Catholics were permitted to serve in Parliament. A radical 1832 law granted suffrage to men whose homes could be rented for at least £10 a year, and the unsuccessful ten-year Chartist movement, begun in 1838, aimed to extend voting rights to all males.

The popularity of Evangelicalism was ebbing by the end of the century, with the advance of urban society and arriving Chinese, Jewish, Italian, German, Irish, and West Indian immigrants. By World War I, a repudiation of Evangelicalism was in full swing in Britain, and the fear and anger (not to mention racism) of Mrs. Mortimer's geography books apparently strained the bounds of good taste until they went out of print. Still, it's only fair to note that Mrs. Mortimer's prejudices, while shocking today, were both widely held and fit to print when she published them. Encyclopedias from her era were far more vicious; an 1854 *Encyclopædia Americana* entry on one group of Australian Aborigines is vile enough to shock today's readers right out of our chairs: "They have very disgusting and ape-like features, stand on the lowest step of bodily and mental improvement, and live in a savage state, without laws and without religion . . . Their deep sunk eyes betray a rude and malicious spirit, and sometimes, though rarely, a stupid good humor."

Any shock value of the milder *Countries of Europe Described* and its two sequels lies mainly in their lack of purple Victorian frills, which otherwise would timestamp their prejudices to 1850s rural England. Writing for eight-year-old kids, Mrs. Mortimer exercised a poetic license only in the rarest moments of weakness, as when she mused on the name of Australia's Botany Bay: "It reminds us not of roses, but of rogues; not of violets, but of violent men; not of lilies, but of villains." I like to imagine the author fanning herself woozily as she pens these words. I hope she gave herself the rest of the day off.

"No doubt," Edwyn Bevan wrote in the *Times* in 1933, "to-day great objection would be felt to some of the pictures put by my aunt a century ago before a small child's mind—the unsparing description of the horrors of hell." The *New Yorker* profile, written seventeen years later, was more forgiving: "If today we see only the humor (or the pathos) of the sadism that ran like a dark thread through her books, it is only fair to add that she was considered in her day to be uniquely successful in communicating with the child mind."

Mrs. Mortimer seemed to understand the value of her own books, even as they began falling out of favor. In 1867, one published critique led her to wax philosophical: "*The Quarterly* has indeed made me look foolish, but I always knew that the language of the nursery must appear ridiculous to the learned. The Testament has been translated into Piccaninny language for the blacks, and if that language save souls, who shall object?"

Clearly, she was a single-minded writer, but her salty sentiments aren't entirely responsible for the eventual disappearance of her body of work. If anything, she engineered her own obscurity. *The Peep of Day* was published anonymously, and each book thereafter was attributed to "the Author of 'The Peep of Day.'" Even the calligraphic ledger of the 1871 Census of England and Wales reveals her modesty; she identified herself to her interviewer not as an author but merely as an "annuitant"—a pensioner.

My crush on this complex woman, I confess, began to get serious. My sentiments had intensified over a slow evolution as mundane as anything you'd witness in a junior-high-school homeroom. An initial spark of scorn and amusement had escalated into curiosity, then fascination, then sympathy—and before I knew it, I couldn't stop thinking about her. I knew she deserved an audience again, and despite any salvation that she hopefully found in prayer, I knew she'd need to be saved by someone on earth. Like any dutifully optimistic lover, I knew I'd be the one to rescue Mrs. Mortimer. But first I'd need to find her.

WHEN MRS. MORTIMER SETTLED in 1862 at Rivulet House, her ramshackle retirement estate in West Runton, the escape from her own grim life must have felt strange and uplifting. "The country round was romantic, undulating, heathery, and woody; the air soft and sweet when the wind was not east," her niece wrote in her biography. "She was delighted with the fine air and beautiful scenery, and found great solace in solitary rambles. There were plenty of simple poor to visit and relieve, and there was pleasant society." Even Mrs. Mortimer, having chosen a pious and unhappy life, allowed herself to betray a tiny bit of sunny good cheer two months after arriving, when she wrote in a letter to a relative:

> Few countries like this for beauty and freshness. How much I should like to have you and your little ones with me when I visit the beach after breakfast with a train of children—the baby carried by four in a plaid down the stairs which we have cut in the steep cliff; he is so happy among the stones and sands that it is hard to get him up again.

Today, the area around the tidy coastal town of Sheringham is still undulating and heathery, though probably a good deal more suburban and well-heeled than it used to be. But glimpses of ancient East Anglia remain. At the bottom of a hill a mile inland from the choppy North Sea, the southbound B1157 abruptly switches from being the two-lane Holt Road into being a narrow street called The Street. To navigate the intersection on foot, I had to scrape my back against the pebbled wall of an ancient cottage and scale it like a secret agent; there's no shoulder at the corner of Holt Road and The Street to shield pedestrians from scampering Mini Coopers. But once I'd rounded the corner and passed the brooding Red Lion Free House (with its surprisingly jaunty blackboard sign: "KEEP SMILING"), I could see the fourteenth-century Upper Sheringham All Saints Church looming ahead. Mrs. Mortimer, I knew, was somewhere out there in the cemetery.

It was a mild Thursday afternoon in March, with white clouds sailing across the sky, and the tilted headstones cast dramatic shadows over the grass. After creaking the gate open, I noticed that the deserted graveyard stretched far into the distance, which shouldn't have surprised me, seeing as the church's doors opened sometime around 1322. The walking paths creasing the churchyard were patrolled by large, unfamiliar birds—pheasants? grouses?—and throughout the disorderly rows, most of the headstones were faded past legibility. Some were listing badly, and many had already keeled over entirely, pinned to the ground by grass and weeds.

I'd assumed that Mrs. Mortimer's grave would be easy to find. Her adopted son, Lethbridge Charles E. Moore, had "served this cure of souls" between 1861 and 1892, according to a banner inside the church; surely she got preferential treatment. Outside, though, the names of two prominent local clans, the Peggs and the Upchers, made a particularly strong showing, but Mrs. Favell Lee Mortimer hadn't revealed herself by the time the shadows began to lengthen.

SHERINGHAM IS A SMALL TOWN, but not too small to have its own museum, whose curator and historian, Peter Brooks, met me at the building's front door on Friday morning. Brooks is tall and angular, a long-retired environmental health officer whose wispy light-brown hair sprouts from the crown of his head. He had never heard of Mrs. Mortimer when I'd first phoned him, a month earlier, but by the time I'd arrived in town, he'd already spent some time exploring the cemetery, searching for her grave. He, too, had come up short.

Brooks introduced me to Jeremy Johnson, a bookish researcher in his thirties, and they briefly gossiped about a London financier who'd shown up in town several days earlier to buy herself a weekend home, forking over a £300,000 check. This was relatively big news; not much has happened in Sheringham since Mrs. Mortimer was buried at the old church. A decade after her death, the first of two railways arrived, turning Mrs. Mortimer's isolated fishing-and-farming district into a tourist boomtown of golf courses and gloomy Victorian beach-side hotels. Since then, Sheringham's last truly exciting moment was in January 1915, when a cottage off Wyndham Street became the first spot in Britain to get bombed by a German zeppelin. (The bomb shattered the roof and landed, without detonating, on a hastily vacated kitchen chair.)

I told Johnson we were on the lookout for Rivulet House. He'd never heard of it, but it didn't take him more than twenty minutes to pull up a nineteenth-century map of West Runton with a notation, next to "Holy Trinity Ch.," for "Rivulet Ho." Comparing it with an aerial photograph of the coastal Cromer Road, parallel to the shore-line, he pinpointed Rivulet House at the corner of Water Lane, which leads to the beach. I could walk there along the cliffs, he said, in less than an hour.

Halfway through my stroll, in an intermittent drizzle, I found a steep wooden cliffside staircase. I can't imagine Mrs. Mortimer and her young friends navigating it with a baby in a blanket—I was amazed to make it down without twisting an ankle—and the beach, it turned out, was a carpet of round gray stones, with a colossal wall of black peat behind it and crashing waves in front. It's hardly an ideal spot for a game of volleyball, but Mrs. Mortimer made a routine of visiting every day after breakfast with a caravan of orphans and pets.

Clacking over the smooth stones, I recalled with alarm a cheerful anecdote in Mrs. Mortimer's *Reading Without Tears,* volume II, describing the day in April 1864 when she tried to give her donkey a swimming lesson. Accompanied by six children, she'd driven to the beach in a donkey cart, and after receiving three letters from a passing postman, she apparently decided that the donkey really ought to learn the breaststroke. She covered the terrified animal's eyes with a shawl and ordered the girls to lead it in, but they dropped the rein, and her pet floated out into the waves. Two quick-thinking fishermen in a rowboat heard the girls' screams and dragged the sputtering animal ashore. Mrs. Mortimer's three letters were lost at sea.

Rivulet House witnessed several of Mrs. Mortimer's Monty Pythonesque experiments in animal nursing. On the occasion of the hundredth anniversary of *The Peep of Day* in 1933, her nephew Edwyn Bevan described her faulty methodology in *The Times* of London:

> She could not believe that it was good for her parrot never to rest its back, and when she took it to bed with her compelled it by slaps to lie on its back. The unhappy bird died, family tradition asserts, from being washed with soap and water and dried before the kitchen fire. . . . The lamb was also subject to sea-bathing; the problems of drying its soaked fleece my aunt solved with characteristic ingenuity: she had it left buried for a time in the sand with only its nose protruding.

Was Mrs. Mortimer insane? "It is possible," Rosalind Constable conceded in her *New Yorker* profile, "that at the end of her life some degree of softening of the brain may have accounted for her eccentricities." Speaking of eccentricities: a digression here—but a good one.

It's hard to imagine someone more poorly suited to being Mrs. Mortimer's biographer, let alone her grandniece, than Rosalind Constable, who, according to her caretaker and close friend, the children's writer Jennifer Owings Dewey, was the vodka-swilling, iconoclastic lesbian daughter of a Nazi-sympathizing aristocratic London mother. Constable detested her mother's beliefs and snuck off to Hollywood in 1934, when she was twenty-seven. As an arts journalist in Manhattan in the late 1940s, she became one of American media's first professional coolhunters, getting paid to keep the editors of Time Inc. apprised of the Beats, Pop Art, and Elvis Presley. Her avant-garde circle included Patricia Highsmith, Allen Ginsberg, Sylvia Plath, Lee Krasner, Willem de Kooning, Richard Diebenkorn, and Andy Warhol, who called her "the den mother of Pop." In 1995, even as she was ailing in a Santa Fe nursing home, Constable was still guzzling stout, Dewey says, and managed to seduce her elderly roommate. I'm sure her great-aunt would've approved.

Once I'd reached Cromer Road and Water Lane, I couldn't tell from my maps which building, if any, had been Mrs. Mortimer's. The place looked like an unassuming country club. A small restaurant, the Village Inn, shared the parking lot with a complex of handsome red-brick apartment houses with tall chimneys and peaked roofs, but nothing here looked like it might have already been falling apart in 1861. I asked two residents, white-haired women walking large, athletic-looking dogs, if they'd ever heard of Rivulet House. They smiled, shook their heads, and walked on.

Later that afternoon, I met Peter Brooks at his house on Abbey Road, and after serving a cup of tea in his living room, he put on a jacket and a houndstooth cap and drove us to the back gate of the Upper Sheringham All Saints Church. We paced through rows of graves, nudging weeds with our shoes to read the blurry inscriptions. Although I had a record of the text on Mrs. Mortimer's monument,

Brooks must have known that actually finding the monument would be a daunting task. He and a team had cleared all the weeds in the vast churchyard seven or eight years earlier, he told me, and I understood his implication: His landscaping efforts might have been the first in decades, or longer. Many of the oldest stones in the yard, he guessed, were probably themselves buried beneath the grass.

At least Brooks could answer one question. "Peter, these birds, walking around—are they grouses?"

"Pheasants," said Brooks. "Grouses live in Scotland."

Brooks, I decided, was kindly trying to avoid telling me that we weren't going to find Mrs. Mortimer that day. Once we'd given up on our mission, he gave me a brief tour of the handsome church, and then he drove us back to the center of Sheringham, pointing out the house that the Germans had bombed. We rode slowly past a public rest room, and he smiled proudly: "Now, this, as far as I'm aware, is the only gents' in the world decorated with stained-glass windows."


THE WEEKEND I VISITED SHERINGHAM, the *Financial Times* ran a story that might have interested Mrs. Mortimer. "Meet the neighbours," ran the headline. "Traditional stereotypes of national character are often out of date, outlandish and outrageously inaccurate. But sometimes they can be uncomfortably true." The article explored the etymologies of five enduring Euro archetypes: how the Spanish became fiery, macho matadors, and how the Swedes became either "dour, Lutheran conservatives" or "communists in Volvos." How the Italians "feign exaggerated gaiety," how the French resist their encroaching multiculturalism, how even the fishermen of Greece are wine-dark philosophers.

Reading the story, it finally dawned on me that the endurance of sweeping cultural stereotypes has a valuable place in our lives. We all paint broad strokes of people we've never met and places we've never seen, based on what we've read and heard and witnessed on TV. Of course, we make such judgments at our peril, but hoary clichés persist and survive because we find them useful. Often, when we want to know how to think about or engage with a representative of an unfamiliar culture, stereotypes are all we have to start with. I remember one morning ten years ago in London, when I told a Jamaican-born cabbie that I was visiting from Chicago. He asked me two questions: if I knew Michael Jordan and (more cautiously) if I owned a gun. A gun—of course! *Chicago! Michael Jordan, Al Capone, bang-bang!*

Mrs. Mortimer's geography books, while giving us a transparent look into Victorian prejudices, are darkly amusing wherever her declarations counter the things we think we know. "Nothing useful is well done in Sweden," she asserts. "The carpenters and the blacksmiths are very clumsy in their work." (True or false? That depends on how you feel about your Saab 9-3 convertible, or your Billy bookshelves from Ikea.) Still, the apparent conventional wisdom of the 1850s—that the "merry" Irish are "fond of drinking," that the Chinese "are quiet, and orderly, and industrious," that the Jews "try in every way to get money," that "the poor people of Mexico cannot bear working"—are still ugly, horrifying, disturbingly familiar. How many centuries have these offensive clichés existed, anyway? How did they get to be so ingrained, so widely accepted, that we still have to fend them off like flies? If Mrs. Mortimer were writing today, what would she tell young readers about Arabs, Iraqis, Palestinians, Israelis, Japanese, Germans, Mexicans, Americans?

"Who are you? It doesn't matter," read a reassuring 1993 article in *Colors* magazine, compiling ethnic insults the world over. "Somewhere in the world a total stranger has an ugly name for you." To white South Africans, *Colors* noted, a black South African is a *kaffir*, a heathen. White people are *caca jumu* (yellow shit) in Haiti and blue-eyed devils in black America; Africans in Germany are *Dachpappe*, tar-paper. In Cambodia, a Vietnamese person is a *yuon*, a savage. Nordics in Japan are *keto* (hairy white barbarians); Mediterraneans in Germany, *Knoblauchfresser* (garlic-eaters); Tibetans in Nepal, *bhotia* (peasants). Indonesians call the Chinese *babi sipit*, narrow-eyed pigs. New Guineans call Melanesians *arse bilong sospan*: burnt-saucepan butt.

Such epithets might have shocked Mrs. Mortimer, whose books reveal not so much outright hatred as scornful pity for those who ate, dressed and worshipped in unfamiliar ways. Today, we barely recognize her scornful pity ourselves. Even as my own reactions to Mrs. Mortimer's work swung from laughter to offense to astonishment to bemusement, I tried to give her a fair shake, sticking as closely as possible to the texts of the first editions (which were often updated with newer information in later years), and editing for brevity while sidestepping most lengthy, digressive anecdotes about individual missionary expeditions. The combination of these factors accounts for the absence of those sixty pages on Madagascar. And I was equally sorry to lose her wild-eyed view of Melbourne ("This is the WORST city to live in of the three cities of Australia . . . There is not a city in the world where there is so much drunkenness"), dating to the 1851 gold rush that apparently missed the first edition's deadline.

Perhaps I've also tried subconsciously to protect Mrs. Mortimer from herself. After all, 150 years after her books were first published, her views seem difficult for us to accept or understand. We've moved beyond such thinking. We live in a multicultural world, and we reject the tired prejudices that inform her writing.

Right? Well . . . it's nice to think so, but the overwhelming evidence suggests otherwise. Even if you consider yourself part of a global society, surrounded by equally open-minded, multicultural friends, our diligent media constantly disclose the wisdom of public figures who should perhaps learn more from today's opportunities to travel the world quickly and easily.

Barring that, they should at least know better than to free-associate in front of a bank of microphones. Maybe Mrs. Mortimer, who almost never left England, would've nodded gravely at the remark of Toronto's then-mayor Mel Lastman, explaining in 2001 his trepidation for an upcoming official visit to Kenya: "What the hell would I want to go to a place like Mombassa? . . . I just see myself in a pot of boiling water, with all these natives dancing around me." Or the deep thoughts of Italy's tourism minister, Stefano Stefani, in 2003: "We know the Germans well, these stereotyped blondes with ultranationalist pride, indoctrinated since way back when to feel top of the class at any price . . . I have never considered the Germans to be endowed with a particularly refined sense of humor." Or Russian politician Ivan Rybkin, who, toward the end of his 2004 challenge to Vladimir Putin's presidential seat, disappeared for five days, and then resurfaced to offer reporters a baffling, beautiful little pearl: "Tyranny is tyranny. Tyranny in Africa is tyranny, only there, they eat people." Or Lt. Gen. William Boykin, the U.S. Defense Department's deputy undersecretary for intelligence, telling a rapt fundamentalist audience in 2003 how he defeated a Somalian Muslim adversary: "You know what I knew—that my God was bigger than his. I knew that my God was a real God, and his was an idol."

Take heart. It's only been 156 years since Mrs. Mortimer published *The Countries of Europe Described*, and only 146 since Charles Darwin published *On the Origin of Species*. Evolution takes time.

*TODD PRUZAN*

*BROOKLYN, NEW YORK, 2004*

*THE*

# CLUMSIEST

# PEOPLE

*IN*

# EUROPE.

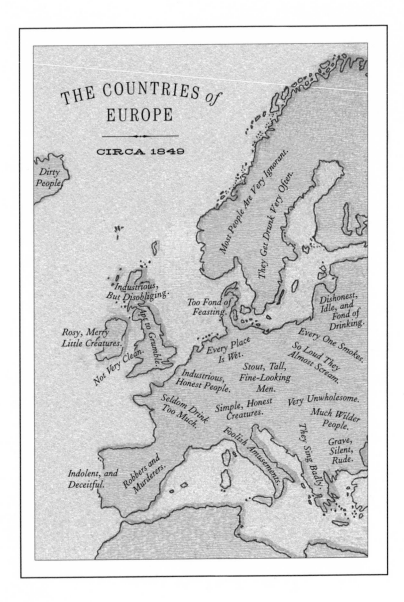

## PART I

# THE
# CLUMSIEST
# PEOPLE
# IN
# EUROPE;

SELECTIONS FROM

*The Countries of
Europe Described,*

with Anecdotes and
Numerous Illustrations,

1849.

# *ENGLAND.*

In the late 1840s, Queen Victoria's Britain was ensconced in a painful adolescence, shaking itself awake from centuries of manors, mead, and jousts, and entering a pit of smoke, filth, disease, and seven-year-old garment workers. Progress wasn't universally unbearable—seven-year-olds were banned from coal mines after 1842, for one thing—and Prime Minister Sir John Peel's 1846 repeal of the 485-year-old Corn Laws brought some prosperity, allowing grain imports during a failed wheat harvest (and worsening the Irish potato famine). The ten-year-old Chartist movement ground to a halt in 1848, and Karl Marx, a Russian-Jewish dissident, settled in London the next year. William Makepeace Thackeray published *Vanity Fair* in 1848, and Charles Dickens's *David Copperfield* came out in 1850. The Brontë sisters issued a one-two punch in 1847 with *Wuthering Heights* and *Jane Eyre*. Sir Edward Frankland discovered amyl alcohol in 1849; Arthur Albright invented phosphorous matches in 1852.

WHAT COUNTRY do you love best? Your *own* country. I know you do. Every child loves his own country best.

Let us talk together about England.

What sort of a land is it? There are green fields, and shady lanes, and white cottages with little gardens.

There are birds which sing sweetly—nightingales and goldfinches, larks and linnets. But is not the robin your favourite bird; not because it has a pretty red breast, but because it comes in winter to the window to be fed?

Now let us speak of the people who live in England.

How do the poor people dress? The men wear cloth coats and beaver hats; the women wear gowns and aprons of cotton, and straw bonnets, and woollen shawls.

In what sort of cottages do they live?

Some cottages are made of planks of wood nailed together; they are cold, because the wind blows in through the chinks. Some are made of bricks, and small stones, and they are very comfortable.

What is the character of the English? What sort of people are they? They are not very pleasant in company, because they do not like strangers, nor taking much trouble. They like best being at home, and this is right. They are very much afraid of being cheated; therefore they are careful and prudent, and slow to trust people till they know them. They are cold in their manners, yet they will often do kind actions. They are too fond of money, as well as of good eating and drinking. They are often in low spirits, and are apt to grumble, and to wish they were richer than they are, and to speak against the rulers of the land. Yet they might be the happiest people in the world, for there is no country in which there are so many Bibles.

❖ ❖ ❖ ❖ ❖

## LONDON.

THIS IS THE NAME of the chief town of England. There is no city in Europe that has so many people in it.

The streets are crowded with people looking very busy. There are a great many shops, with beautiful things at the windows to tempt the people to buy.

London is full of buyers and sellers, and many people in it are very rich.

But many are very poor.

The rich people live in wide streets and in large squares. It is pleasant to live in a square, for it has a garden in the middle with iron railings around it.

Is London a pleasant city? No; because there is so much fog and so much smoke. This makes it dark and black. Yet the streets where rich people live are kept clean, and the maid in each house washes the steps of her master's house every morning.

Is London a pretty city? No; because it is not built by the sea-side or on high hills. Yet it has two beautiful churches—called St. Paul's and Westminster Abbey—and it has some beautiful parks where ladies and gentlemen drive and walk, and where even poor children play under the shady trees.

But the poor people live in narrow alleys or streets, and in close places called courts, into which no carriages can drive.

There are schools also for little ragged children—such as could not go to a neat Sunday-school. These children have been taught at home to steal, and lie, and swear; but some of them listen to their kind teachers while they are telling them about God, and Christ, and heaven and hell. At first these rude children push each other about, and laugh, and make jokes; but soon they learn to sit still and attend.

❖ ❖ ❖ ❖ ❖

## MANCHESTER.

NEXT TO LONDON this is the largest town in England. There it is that those cotton prints are made which so many women and children wear.

There are large houses there full of great machines, and men and women making calico and cotton print. These houses are called factories.

And are there any children in these large houses? Yes; but none younger than eight years old. Once very young children used to work there, but a kind nobleman called Lord Ashley pitied the poor little creatures, and now a law is made to prevent their working. Children of eight years old begin to work in the cotton-mills, but only for six hours in the day.

---

# WALES.

The Welsh language suffered a slow decline throughout the 19th century: By 1841, just two thirds of England's western principality spoke the local tongue, and the use of English was spreading far more quickly than Welsh. The population almost doubled between 1811 and 1851, to nearly 1.2 million—of whom 808 men and 202 women were cooling their heels in jail. Riots sparked by food shortages and highway tolls unsettled the region in the 1840s, but iron production was booming. By 1848, 207 furnaces were belching out some 722,800 tons of the stuff annually, nearly triple the production of 1825. By midcentury, Wales supported ten religious magazines, a weekly, and a nondenominational quarterly.

IT LIES CLOSE BY the side of England. The people in it are called the Welsh.

What sort of people are they?

Their figures are short and stout—they have broad faces with fresh colours. They are passionate when offended, but very honest and industrious. The women will even knit as they walk along to market. There are not nearly as many thieves in Wales as there are in England.

The Welsh are fond of music. Their favourite instrument is the harp. You may sometimes see an aged man, with silver hair, singing an old Welsh song while he plays upon his harp.

Though the Welsh are not very clean, they make their cottages look clean by white-washing them every year, and sometimes they white-wash the pig-sties too.

*THIS IS THE MOST BEAUTIFUL CITY*
*IN THE WORLD.*

# SCOTLAND.

In 1851, Scotland's 2,888,742 locals included 161 soap-boilers, 531 cork-cutters, and the proprietors of 167 distilleries (as well as 223 brewers of "strong beer"). Paper production nearly doubled between 1841 and 1851, to 31,723,001 pounds, and the 795 miles of railway in 1849 had stretched to 1,243 miles by the end of 1857.

**THE COUNTRY.**——Just at the north of England, there is a country called Scotland. It looks like the head of England. It is a large head certainly, but you can almost see the nose, and the chin, and the bunch of hair on the top; at least you can fancy that you see them.

Is Scotland like England?

No—it is more beautiful. It has not as many trees as England has, but then it has very high hills, higher than any hills in England, and larger lakes, and more streams and water-falls.

One day a traveller said to a Scotchman, "Does it always rain, as it does now?" "No," replied the man, "it snaws sometimes."

He said "snaws," instead of "snows," for the poor Scotch speak their words very broad.

**FOOD.** ——The poor people are content with very coarse food. Instead of eating wheaten bread, they often eat oaten cakes. You must not think these cakes are nicer than bread, for they are hard and bitter.

There is also a dish called haggis, made of oatmeal, fat, liver, and bacon, all boiled together in a skin; and there is another dish called hotch-potch, in which all sorts of food are boiled together and made into soup. Greens and eggs help to make out the poor Scotchman's dinner. It would be better if he only drank water with his simple food; but the Scotch are very fond of whiskey.

The rich people have a great many nice things for breakfast, especially a sort of jam called marmalade. They also eat very rich cakes, which may be kept for six months without spoiling: but such dainties are very unwholesome.

**APPEARANCE.**——The Scotch are tall, and strong, with large bones. Their faces are broad, and their cheek-bones high, their eyes and hair are light. They look grave and thoughtful.

**CHARACTER.**——The Scotch are very wise and sensible. They love reading. A traveller stopped at an inn, where there was only one bed for him, and that a very poor one, in a hole in the wall; yet he found that the innkeeper had a great many books, and amongst them several Bibles, also an Encyclopedia, a book which explains how everything is made; and this book had cost three guineas. The blacksmith, too, in the village, had two hundred books, some of them about religion, and some about animals and plants. Yet it is sad to say, this clever smith liked drinking, and asked the traveller for some money to buy whiskey.

One of the chief faults of the Scotch, is the love of whiskey. Another fault is the love of money. They often ask more than they ought, and are very slow to give.

They are industrious, but disobliging. They will not take much trouble to please strangers. They are not as clean as English people, and they let their books be covered with dust, and even black with soot.

They are very grave, and not fond of jokes; however, they like music, and can sing some very pretty songs; but you would not like the sound of their bag-pipes. The noise is almost as ugly as the creaking of a door, or the squalling of cats.

◇ ◇ ◇ ◇ ◇

## EDINBURGH.

THE CHIEF TOWN of Scotland. This is the most beautiful city in the world. What makes it so beautiful? Its green hill with the castle at the top. As you walk in the fine broad streets of Edinburgh, whenever you look up, you see this hill and its castle, and you admire them, and say, "How grand, how beautiful!"

All the streets are not broad. There are streets so narrow that two people can scarcely pass along, and friends might easily shake hands out of the opposite windows. How dark and dismal the houses must be! A right name is given to these narrow streets. They are called "closes." They are close indeed. The houses are twelve or fourteen stories high, and are crowded with very dirty poor people.

◇ ◇ ◇ ◇ ◇

## GLASGOW.

THIS CITY is larger than Edinburgh, yet it is not so famous, be-cause kings have never lived here, as they once did in Edinburgh. There are a great many places in Glasgow, where cotton is made into calico, and muslin, and they are called manufactories; and there are a great many rich people who live in fine houses. But the smoke from the manufactories, makes the city unpleasant. The cottages all round, where the poor people live, are very dirty and miserable. Unlike the tall houses of Edinburgh, these have no rooms up stairs, and they look more like pig-sties than cottages. Ragged children come out of them, and beg of the travellers who pass by.

# *IRELAND.*

Not surprisingly, 1850s statistics paint a bleak picture of life on the island. A sustained potato crop failure (accompanied by outbreaks of typhoid fever, cholera and dysentery) starved a million Irish and began driving millions of refugees to Britain and North America for the rest of the century and beyond. Ireland blamed the non-interventionist British, supplying little aid or financial relief during the blight, for the sustained famine, which slashed the 1841 population of 8.2 million to 6.5 million a decade later. Queens Colleges of Belfast, Cork, and Galway opened in 1849; the country's seventy-nine newspapers in 1843 had grown to 140 papers by 1863.

**COUNTRY.**——Ireland, you know, has been called the Emerald Island, because the emerald is a green stone, and the fields of Ireland are very green. And why are they so green? Because it rains so much.
**COTTAGES.**——There are no huts in the world so miserable as the Irish cabins or cottages.

Where is the window? Where is the chimney? There are none. Only one square hole serves for the door, and through it the smoke goes out and the light comes in. Inside there is no floor—only the damp earth. The rain comes down upon pig and all through the holes in the roof. In one corner there is a heap of straw with a blanket over it: it is a bed; in the other the pig lies on another heap of straw still more dirty.

All the cottages are not so miserable as this; some have a window and a chimney, and some have inside one or two chairs, two or three plates, and a bedstead.
**FOOD.**——Potatoes are the food. Potatoes for breakfast, potatoes for

dinner, and potatoes for supper. There are very poor Irish who only taste meat once a year, that is on Christmas day. They drink milk when they can get it, and often they drink whiskey.

**APPEARANCE.**——Though they live on potatoes, the Irish are a fine strong people. Their complexions are fair and rosy, for the sun is never very hot nor the wind very cold, and the damp mild weather is good for the skin.

**DRESS.**——Rags. This is the dress of the poor Irish. They do not mend their clothes, so the holes get larger and larger. Their coats are made of a gray woollen cloth called "frieze," and they are worn till they drop off the back: first one tail of the coat comes off, then the other, and then the sleeves disappear, till at length nothing but a heap of rags remains.

**SCHOOLS.**——The Irish children are rosy, merry little creatures. They like potato dinners, and care not to run barefoot with their rags fluttering about them, while they call out "Halfpenny, halfpenny," to the passers by. Sometimes they go to school; but an Irish school is a curious sight. There are some schools where poor children are taught under the hedges or a haystack, but as it is always raining it is unpleasant to have no roof.

The Irish have a language of their own, but they learn English in school. In some parts of Ireland the people have forgotten their own language, and speak nothing but English.

**CHARACTER.**——What sort of people are the Irish? The merriest, drollest people in the world. They are very kind and good-natured when pleased, but if affronted, are filled with rage. The poor men are fond of drinking and keeping company with friends; but they often quarrel with them, and then they call them names and throw things at them, and cover them with bruises. You see they are passionate; though they wish to be kind, they forget themselves and act in a wicked manner.

There are not many rich people in Ireland. Those who are rich like best going over to England and living there, and this is one reason why the poor people are so very poor. But there are some ladies and gentlemen who try to make poor people happy, and who have schools for the children.

**RELIGION.**——The Irish say they are Christians, yet most of them will not read the Bible. Is not that strange? Why do they not read it, if they are Christians? Because their ministers tell them not to read it. Why? Because these ministers or priests tell them a great many wrong things, which are not written in the Bible, and they do not want the people to find out the truth.

The religion they teach is called the Roman Catholic religion. It is a kind of Christian religion, but it is a very bad kind.

*ALL THE COTTAGES ARE NOT*
*SO MISERABLE AS THIS.*

If you were to go to a Roman Catholic church, you would see a basin of water near the door. What is it for? It is called "holy water," because the priest has blessed it. Everybody dips his hand in this water, and sprinkles himself with it, and thinks that doing this will keep him from Satan. O how foolish!

❖ ❖ ❖ ❖ ❖

## DUBLIN.

*DUBLIN*, the chief city, is very beautiful.

There are very handsome streets in Dublin; they are broad, and straight, and pleasant to walk in. In London, there are many pretty squares with iron railings round them, and trees, and grass in the middle, where children play by the side of their nurses. But there are much larger squares in Dublin. But Dublin is not beautiful all over. There are parts where the poor people live crowded together in rags, and dirt, and misery. In some houses a dozen people live in every room. How unpleasant that must be!

## FRANCE.

In February 1848, the latest national revolution kicked the pan-European revolts into high gear. February riots relieved King Louis Philippe of his regal duties and extended suffrage to all Frenchmen, who elected Louis Napoleon Bonaparte, nephew of the insecure emperor, to a four-year term as president—which he transitioned into dictatorship in an 1851 coup d'état. Vintners produced 51.6 million hectares of wine in 1848. Composer Héctor Berlioz debuted *Damnation of Faust* in 1846, and Prosper Merimée's *Carmen*, a novel of passion, appeared the following year. In 1851, Jean Foucault proved that Earth spins on an axis, and Henri Giffard introduced balloon flight in 1852. *Le Figaro* hit the streets in 1854.

**COUNTRY AND PEOPLE.**——From England you need only cross the water in a steam boat, and in three hours you will be in France. You will see the same kind of trees and hills that you saw in England, but not the same sort of people. The poor women wear no bonnets nor shawls, but high white caps, long ear-rings, and handkerchiefs very neatly put on. Very few have rosy cheeks, or light hair; they have dark complexions, and dark eyes and hair; they hold up their heads, walk briskly, and look gay and smiling.

The French people are very fond of talking, and they are very fond of company.

Gardens in France are not as pretty as those in England, because the walks are straight, between high smooth hedges of box, or rows of trees, while in England they have winding shrubberies, and green lawns with flower-beds scattered about.

**THE POOR PEOPLE.**——Though France is such a sweet country, yet there are many very poor people there.

Some have a little piece of land of their own, and they plant it with vines, but if the sun does not ripen their grapes (and sometimes it does not), they almost starve.

They do not drink tea and sugar, as they do in England; they have not money enough to buy them. Now and then, when they are sick, they put a little sugar in some water and drink it, but they cannot have it every day.

They very seldom drink too much. In England, it is a common thing for a poor man to get drunk, but it is very uncommon in

France. People sometimes whisper to each other, and say, "That man once got drunk."

The poor women work very hard. They are glad to help their husbands in their own little fields, or to earn money by working out. They may often be seen ploughing or digging, or carrying baskets of manure on their heads.

FOOD.——The rich people are fond of messes of nice things. Their cooks are considered very clever, and even English people who wish to have very fine dinners send for French cooks to live with them. There is no plum-pudding, but cake and fruits instead. A great many sweetmeats and sugarplums are made in France. Boxes of "bonbons" that look very pretty are sent to England; but children who eat many soon spoil their teeth and hurt their health.

CHILDREN.——The parents like to make them little men and women. They take them where they go, keep them up late, and let them eat unwholesome food, and even allow them to talk away before grown-up people, and show how clever they are. Children of five or six years old often dine with company, when they ought to be alone with their papa and mamma, or else in the nursery.

RELIGION.——There is the same religion in France that there is in Ireland—the Roman Catholic.

There are no pews in the churches, but there are chairs heaped up in one corner; and if people want to sit down they hire a chair for a halfpenny. They may sit down in what part of the church they like, and go out and come in when they please, so there is a great deal of confusion and bustle in the churches.

On Sunday evening the French play at all kinds of games, and go to see sights and to hear music, and they meet together to dance.

There are houses in France called Convents. In some of these women live called nuns. They think they please God by shutting themselves up in a home together. But what can the nuns teach?

They teach their little scholars to work, and to sing, and to draw; and also they teach them to worship the Virgin Mary. Protestant parents ought never to send their children to convents to be taught.

GOVERNMENT.——Is there a King of France? The last King left his palace in great haste. There were crowds under his windows, and he was afraid they would burst in. So he left his dinner unfinished on the table; he did not stop to pack up his clothes, but, with his queen on his arm, he hurried through the streets, and got into a carriage and drove off. Where did he go? To England. That is a safe place for French kings.

THE PARENTS KEEP CHILDREN UP LATE,
AND LET THEM EAT UNWHOLESOME FOOD.

CHARACTER.——There are no people so gay and so polite as the French. They do not drink much, nor eat much either. They like being smart, but are not very clean. It is too common in France not to speak truth, for the French pay a great many compliments to please their company, and these compliments are often not true. The French are called witty, for they say things which make people laugh. The French are brave in war. They have fought many battles with the English; but I hope they will fight no more.

❖ ❖ ❖ ❖ ❖

## PARIS.

*IT IS A VERY GAY CITY.* There are a great many pretty shops and finely dressed people. There are large gardens where anybody may walk. But I do not think you would call them pretty, because the walks are straight, with rows of trees on each side.

What they care for most is fine dress. Every week there are new fashions, new shapes for bonnets, and new colours. Pictures are drawn of the fashions and sent to other countries, and English people like to dress as the people do at Paris.

Each family in Paris does not have a whole house to itself. On each floor of a house there is a different family. The rooms are not as comfortable as in England.

# *S P A I N .*

As the kingdom continued to lose colonies to independence throughout Latin America, Queen Isabella II's reign was beset in the 1830s and 1840s by revolts and a bloody civil war at home. In 1839 Isabella, aided by the British, defeated the Carlists, who demanded the rule of her uncle Don Carlos; she survived attempts on her life in 1847 and 1852. The national economy was starting to bloom—its 1849 imports would quadruple by 1862, and the cotton industry was growing rapidly. An eighteen-mile railway, the country's first, connected Barcelona to Mataro in October 1848, and by 1861, fifteen hundred miles of track would be complete. The habanera, a dance in moderate double-time, was the rage of 1850.

**THE COUNTRY.**——Is Spain a beautiful country? Yes, it is very beautiful. There are high mountains, and very wide plains, and fine trees, and a clear blue sky.

There are some men in Spain who act like wolves: there are robbers and murderers there. They hide themselves among the caves in the mountains, and among the thickets in the forests. As you travelled through Spain you would often see black crosses set up by the roadside with some writing upon them. What are these crosses for? Read what is written upon one—"A man named Charles was murdered here in May, 1840." Read what is written upon the next—"A woman, named Julia, and her children, were murdered here in January, 1736." Whenever a person has been murdered by the roadside, a cross is set up to mark the place.

Sometimes, as you went along, you would hear the tinkling of bells, with the deep sound of men's voices singing. You need not fear lest robbers are coming, for *they* make no noise.

Two Spaniards were once walking along the hills, when they saw a whole troop of wolves coming along; one large fierce gray wolf led the way, and the rest followed. The poor men tried to get out of the way, as well as they could. But the first wolf turned that very way, and the rest came after it. The wolf passed by one of the men without noticing him, though it came so near him, that its bristly hair brushed the man's legs. When it came to the other man, it passed by—almost—then turned half round, and snapped at him, without biting him. That was a sign to the pack of wolves to eat him. They understood the sign, and in a few moments tore the man limb from limb, howling all the while most dreadfully, and leaving nothing but bones.

**FOOD.**——The Spaniards take a late supper when they come in from their evening walk, just before they go to bed, which is about eleven. The supper is of stewed beef, and tomatoes, or love-apples, dressed in oil. No wonder they cannot eat much breakfast next morning, for this late supper must hurt their health.

There are a great many olive-trees in Spain, fine spreading trees, and the olive is a little dark round fruit, about the size of a plum. The Spaniards eat it with salt, but the taste is so bitter, I am sure you would not like it.

**COTTAGES.**——Some of the cottages are very miserable indeed. A gentleman travelling amongst the mountains with his guide, came to a village where there were a few black huts. He knocked at the door of one. A man opened it, holding a burning piece of wood in his hand instead of a candle. The gentleman asked to be allowed to sleep in the hut that night. The poor man let him in, and led him first through a room full of straw, then through a stable into the room where the family lived. After providing bacon and eggs for supper, he pointed to a small door in the roof, and told the gentleman he might sleep there upon some clean straw.

"Is there no bed in the cottage?" asked the gentleman.

"No," replied the poor man, "I never slept in a bed in all my life, nor did my children, nor did my father and mother before me. We sleep on the hearth by the fire, or else among the cattle in the stable."

**AMUSEMENTS.**——The favourite amusement of the young people is dancing. They are very fond of playing on the guitar, and singing songs as they play. Very few people like reading or any useful employment.

But the Spaniards are not only idle, they are very cruel. They delight in bull-fights. There is a large building in every town for fighting bulls. The people are glad when they see the bull driven in.

When the bull has been tormented for a long while, a man on horseback enters with a sword to kill him. While the bull puts down its head, in order to try to hurt with its horns, the man pierces its neck with his sword. As soon as he has done it, the people give a shout of joy. The bull does not die immediately, but runs backwards and forwards, in an agony, till he drops down dead.

And can women like to see such bloody sights? Yes, they do,—and priests, who ought to show the people what is right, are pleased to view these wicked deeds.

◇　◇　◇　◇　◇

## MADRID.

*THIS CITY IS BUILT* just in the middle of Spain.

The king, who chose Madrid for his chief city, made a foolish choice; for it is far from the sea, and there is no great river near, only a little stream, so that ships cannot come near it. It is built also on a high plain, where very cold winds blow. It would not be well to go to Madrid in winter, it is so very windy, and there are no good plans for keeping the houses warm. In summer it is very hot.

**HOUSES.**——The window of the lowest room has iron bars, to hinder thieves from getting in, and this makes it look like a prison. But the people live in the upper rooms, and keep lumber and stores in the lower.

**DRESS, AND APPEARANCE.**——The Spaniards are rather short and thin. Their hair and eyes are black, their skin is dark, and their cheeks pale, and their countenance is grave and sad. They walk very slowly, and hold up their heads. The women are very graceful.

**THE PRISON.**——It was a horrible place. There were no beds, but

*THE SPANIARDS ARE NOT ONLY IDLE,*
*THEY ARE VERY CRUEL.*

only horse-cloths spread on the floor. The darkest, and dirtiest of all the dungeons, was one in which the little thieves were locked up,—poor boys who had scarcely a rag to cover them.

But amongst the dirty, and the ragged prisoners, some very gaily-dressed men were seen. They wore shirts of snow-white linen with wide sleeves, waistcoats of blue or green silk with silver buttons, silk stockings, crimson girdles, and gay silk handkerchiefs of many colours round their heads. Who were these men? Robbers,—the boldest,—the proudest,—the greatest of the robbers. They had wicked friends in Madrid, who gave them fine clothes.

◇ ◇ ◇ ◇ ◇

SEVILLE.

*THIS CITY IS BUILT* on that fine river, the Guadalquiver.

The streets are so narrow that a person walking in the middle might touch the houses on both sides. If you enter, you go through a passage till you come to a little court behind, with rooms all round. The people sit in this court in summer-time. It is pleasanter than in-doors.

But it would not be pleasant to live in Seville, because the people are very wicked. There is no city where there are so many bull-fights, for such strong bulls feed on the banks of the Guadalquiver. And at what time are the bull-fights? On Sunday afternoons!

**CHARACTER.**——They are not like the French, lively and talkative: they are grave and silent. They are not active like the Scotch, but cold and distant; nor fond of home like the English, but fond of company. Yet they are cruel, and sullen, and revengeful. They are very proud. The poor are as proud as the rich. They think no nation, and no language is like their own. It is true their language is the finest in Europe, but there are very few wise books written in it.

---

# *PORTUGAL.*

With the glory of colonialism long faded—its former colony Brazil declared independence in 1822, and most of its remaining holdings were in Africa and Asia—Portugal in the late 1840s was not at its most productive. Although the decade saw the foundation of the first national railroad, wine and olive oil were the only industries of much significance. Lisbon was still recovering from the 1755 earthquake-tsunami disaster that leveled 80 percent of the city. Queen Maria II da Gloria put down an April 1846 insurrection in the northern provinces, and England, France and Spain aided her in quelling civil war in 1847.

**THE COUNTRY.**——Portugal is very much like Spain; the people are alike, the customs are alike, the plants and animals are alike, and though the languages are not the *same*, there is a great likeness between them. Yet there is some difference between these countries.

What? Though the Portuguese are indolent, like the Spaniards, they are not so grave, and sad, and silent. They are proud like the Spaniards, but they are more deceitful. They have black eyes, and hair, and dark complexions like the Spaniards, but they have whiter teeth, for they never smoke, and it is smoking paper cigars which spoils the teeth in Spain.

But though the Portuguese do not smoke, they have another bad habit, they take snuff continually,—the poor as well as the rich,—the young as well as the old.

The Portuguese language is not as beautiful as the Spanish, it has more hissing sounds, and is spoken in harsh and squeaking tones.

No people in Europe are as clumsy and awkward with their hands as the Portuguese. It is curious to see how badly the carpenters make boxes, and the smiths make keys. The carts are very ill-made; they are drawn by two oxen, and as they move slowly along, the wheels make a loud creaking noise, which almost stuns people of other countries; but the Portuguese do not mind the sound, and say it is of use, for then there will be no danger of two carts meeting in the narrow roads.

Portugal, like Spain, is filled with robbers; the laws are not obeyed, and the wicked men often escape without being punished.

❖  ❖  ❖  ❖  ❖

## LISBON.

SOME PLACES LOOK PRETTY at a distance which look very ugly when you come up to them—Lisbon is one of these places.

If you were to cross the Atlantic in a ship, and to go up the broad river Tagus, you would very soon see Lisbon. It is built just at the mouth of the river upon some hills. When first you see Lisbon, the white houses glittering in the sun, the balconies adorned with flowers and shrubs, and the lovely orange groves,—you cry out, "What a beautiful city!" But when you have landed on the shore, and begin to walk in the streets, you do not like it so well; for the streets are not swept clean like those of Madrid—they are full of litter and rubbish;—and troops of dirty dogs are seen on every side, and very unpleasant smells come from the houses, and in most of the streets there is no pavement. But if you do not like Lisbon when you walk in it, you like it worse when you live there, because it is full of stinging insects; at night the musquitoes annoy you every moment. Sometimes snakes find their way into the houses and frighten children very much. But there are worse creatures than snakes in Lisbon—there are many murderers there. It is believed that many dead bodies are thrown by wicked people into the Tagus.

Is there nothing pleasant in Lisbon? There is one thing very beautiful—it is the Aqueduct. Near Lisbon there is a deep valley, and there is a very high bridge with five high arches over this valley, and the water runs *through* the bridge, not under it. This aqueduct is the finest in Europe and in the world.

But what are those heaps of stones?—those large heaps of great stones? They look like churches and houses fallen down. And so they are; for about a hundred years ago a great earthquake shook Lisbon, and threw down many of the buildings, and killed numbers of the people. This dreadful day can never be forgotten.

*NO PEOPLE IN EUROPE ARE AS CLUMSY
AND AWKWARD WITH THEIR HANDS
AS THE PORTUGUESE.*

# *R U S S I A .*

The expansionist ambitions of Czar Nicholas I, reigning since 1825, led the country to crush anti-empire revolts in Poland in 1830 and Hungary in 1849. (In 1853, Nicholas would enter into the Crimean War against the Ottoman Empire: a massive Balkan and Black Sea land-grab that ended in Russia's defeat in 1856, after Nicholas's death.) In the 1840s and 1850s, the country saw dramatic increases of schools and (heavily censored) publications. Nikolai Gogol published *Dead Souls* in 1842, and the anarchist Mikhail Bakunin first advanced the nihilist movement in 1850. The empire's 1862 population was nearly seventy-four million.

R*USSIA IS THE LARGEST COUNTRY* in the world.

Is Russia a pleasant country? You shall tell me whether you think it is pleasant.

In winter all is covered with one vast sheet of snow. There are very few people walking along the road—but instead of people there are wild beasts hid in the forests. What wild beasts? Bears and wolves.

Wolves are bolder than bears. They like to live near villages, amongst the brushwood and the bushes. One wolf will not dare to attack a man, but when he finds a child straying alone in a wood, he generally carries him off.

DRESS.——The men let their hair grow long, and, when they are at work, bind it up to keep it out of their eyes. They wear also long beards. The women dress in a very clumsy manner. Their gowns hang loose around them, without any band round the waist; they wear large sheepskin boots that make their legs look like elephants'. The gentlemen wear fur cloaks.

**FOOD.**——The favourite drink is called "kwas." It is made of barley-meal, honey, and salt, mixed together in water, and then warmed for many hours in the oven. This is a wholesome drink, but you would not like it at all.

The poor people eat black bread made of rye. They drink tea as we do: in every cottage there is a copper kettle and teapot. I wish they loved no other drink except kwas and tea; but they love brandy too well, and drink it, not in little cups, but in large tumblers, and even give it to their babies to sip.

**THE COTTAGES.**——The Russians live in very miserable dwellings made of trees cut down and laid along the ground, one on top of the other. The windows are very small, and some of them have no glass, but only wooden shutters. In the middle of the room is a large stove that fills it with smoke.

**THE RICH MEN.**——The rich men have very large houses and a great many servants. Though the rooms are large and grand, they are not neat.

There is only a little carpet in one corner; and the walls, instead of being papered, are whitewashed. There are no bells. The men-servants do not need beds to sleep in. They lie in the passages, or take the cushions from the sofas, and sleep on the drawing-room floor.

The rich people are very fond of company; nothing pleases them more than to see some sledges gallopping up to their house. Then they make fine feasts, talk and laugh, sing and dance, from morning till night. The children are allowed to play so much, that they grow up very ignorant. The boys are not taught Latin or Greek, for they are so foolish as to think it too much trouble to learn languages which nobody speaks now.

The Russians are very fond of music and dancing, and the children are very quick in learning to dance and sing; but dancing and singing will not make them wise.

**RELIGION.**——Perhaps you think the Russians are Roman Catholics. No, they are not. Instead of minding the Pope at *Rome*, they follow the religion of *Greece*. It is hard to say which is the better and which is the worse, the Greek or the Roman religion.

The Russians behave very respectfully to the priests: instead of shaking hands with them, they always kiss their hands; but they do not respect them in their hearts, for many of the priests are as fond of drinking as any of the people.

**THE EMPEROR.**——He does whatever he pleases. He often punishes people without telling them what it is for. Sometimes he sends them to a country a great way off, called Siberia. It is in Asia.

Coachmen are sent to Siberia, if they run over a person in the streets. This makes them very careful, but it makes the people very troublesome. Instead of getting out of the way, they will look up at the coachman, and say, "Mind Siberia."

*COACHMEN ARE SENT TO SIBERIA,*
*IF THEY RUN OVER A PERSON IN THE STREETS.*

❖ ❖ ❖ ❖ ❖

## PETERSBURGH.

*THE CHIEF CITY* of Russia is called Petersburgh. And why has it this name? Because it was built by an Emperor called Peter.

There is no city so full of palaces and fine houses, as Petersburgh. The Emperor has a very grand palace called the Winter Palace. It is the largest in Europe, and it is built in the largest square in Europe.

**THE MARKET-PLACES.**——If you want to buy anything in Petersburgh, you had better go to the market-places. There are some shops in the streets, but most of the goods are sold in a market-place. What a large building it is!

There are some very strange things to be seen in the market. Look at those white hares, that appear to be running along the ground, and those cows which never move, and their calves beside them; and those quiet pigs with their little ones. They are all dead, but they are frozen, and therefore they are stiff, and stand upright.

**THE BLACK PEOPLE.**——Who are these? The poor Russians are not black, but fair, with light hair. Why are they called "black?" Because they are very dirty. You will be surprised to hear that these dirty people bathe once a week. On Saturday evening, they may be seen with a towel in one hand, and a birch twig in the other, hurrying to the bathing-houses. In these bathing-houses the people do not dip in water. Large stones are first heated in the stoves; when they are taken out, water is poured upon them, and that fills the room with steam, or vapour. The people lie on the benches, and grow quite hot from the steam. Men come and beat them with their birch twigs, and throw pails of cold water over them. This is thought very pleasant. The Russians are very uneasy if they cannot bathe.

**WINTER IN PETERSBURGH.**——The people run so fast in the streets, that you would think they were running for their lives; and so they are, for if they were to stand still, they would be frozen. Little children cannot go out at all in the midst of winter, but boys who are fast runners can.

**EASTER AT PETERSBURGH.**——On Good Friday, there is a long box placed in the churches, covered with a cloth, and on the cloth the body of the Saviour is painted, with his five bleeding wounds. Numbers of people hasten to the churches to kiss the painted wounds, and many cry and sob. Is it not wrong and foolish to worship an image?

On the morning of Easter Sunday, every one who meets a friend cries out, "Christ is risen," then kisses him, and presses and egg into his hand.

And how does the day end? In feasting and drunkenness. Sometimes all the people in a village are drunk at Easter. The streets of Petersburgh are filled with staggering, reeling drunkards.

❖　❖　❖　❖　❖

## MOSCOW.

*THIS CITY WAS* the chief city of Russia, till Peter the great built Petersburgh.

Moscow is very unlike Petersburgh. Which would you like the best?

I know you would like Moscow the best. It is not so grand as Petersburgh, but it is much more pleasant. You would find it very amusing to ramble about it. You would see something new at every step.

The most beautiful place in the city is the Kremlin. What is the Kremlin? It is not one building, but many collected together on the top of a hill, and surrounded with walls. What is that great building which looks like many boxes, one on the top of the other, and the smallest at the top? That is the old palace where kings lived long ago. One named Ivan was so cruel as to have men cut up in small pieces while yet alive. At last, in a passion he killed his own son with his iron-pointed staff. His son was in pain for four days, and then he died.

**CHARACTER.**——By this time you must have found out the character of the Russians. The rich people are unjust, and often do not pay their debts; they are fond of feasts and company, but they care little for their servants and poor neighbours.

The poor people are civil, but sly, and dishonest, idle, and fond of drinking.

Yet though the Russians are generally not to be trusted, I have heard of one who acted in a very upright manner.

A lady said to a servant, "Take this money to my daughter." Soon afterwards, the man returned, crying, "I have lost the money, I do not know how. Please forgive me." Six years afterwards, the man appeared, and laid the money at her feet. The lady would not take it, and he would not take it back. Therefore the kind lady put it in the bank to keep it for the poor man's children.

# *I TA L Y .*

In January 1848, Italian states favoring unification and cultural libera-
tion revolted against the ruling Austrian Empire throughout the region.
Between 1848 and 1850, the Austrians crushed the weak new republics
of Piedmont, Rome, Tuscany, and Naples. Of the future Italy's breakaway republics, only Sardinia managed to remain independent, until
Austria's defeat in 1859 led to a unified Italian kingdom centered in
Turin. "Owing to the defective mode of their manufacture," an 1863
Scottish encyclopedia noted, Italy's wines were "unfit for exportation,
as they can neither bear transport, nor do they improve by age."

WHAT A CHANGE it would be for any one to go from the snowy
forests of Russia to the sunny plains of Italy! Italy has often been
called the Garden of Europe.

**PEOPLE.**——What sort of people live in Italy? They are very dark,
because the sun shines so much. They have dark hair and eyes,——not
those bright, merry, black eyes you see in France, but more sad and
thoughtful eyes. They may well be sad, for their country is in a sad
state. It is full of fine houses and palaces——empty and going to de-
cay——but that is not the worst part——the people are ignorant and
wicked.

Their religion is the Roman Catholic.

Their chief amusement is gambling. They play at all sorts of
games; some with cards and some with their fingers; they are always
trying to win each other's money.

There are a great many other foolish amusements in Italy. Sometimes people put on masks, and run about the streets and see whether

anybody can find them out when their faces are hid. Another day everybody takes a candle, and the amusement is to try and blow out other people's candles and keep your own alight. These are very foolish games, especially for grown-up people.

The Italians are very fond of music, and of painting, and of statues. They do not care so much for useful things as they do for beautiful things. The English care more for what is useful. A great many Italian boys go to London. Why do these boys leave their own country to go there? You would not wonder at their going, if you could see what crowds of miserable beggars there are in Italy. It is quite unpleasant to see the poor creatures in troops, clothed in filthy rags, many of them with bad sores, and others with broken backs or legs. They follow strangers about from place to place. When money is given to these poor creatures, they are not as thankful as Irish beggars are.

It is dreadful to think what a number of murders are committed in Italy. Even boys, instead of fighting with their hands, take up stones to throw at each other, and men take out their knives and cut each other.

**HOUSES.**——All day you must keep the blinds down or the sun will scorch you. But may you open them in the evening and enjoy the pure air? No, then you must shut the windows, or the musquitoes will come in and bite you all over.

The houses are very dirty, especially the staircase and the doorway; but the Italians think more of painting their ceilings and placing statues in their halls than of keeping their houses clean. The English think a clean house is better than a pretty one.

**FOOD.**——The favourite food of poor people is macaroni. What is that? It is made of flour and water in the shape of pipes. Macaroni looks like white serpents. There are plenty of stalls in the towns where macaroni is sold, and the poor people in the evening go and buy their supper, and you may see them holding up this serpent-like food and letting it slip down their throats.

**CUSTOMS.**——One very bad custom is burying the poor people in large pits. In the evening the dead bodies in coffins are taken in carts and thrown into a deep hole and covered up.

When a man is condemned to die, instead of being hanged, his head is cut off, and then stuck upon a pole for everybody to see.

❖ ❖ ❖ ❖ ❖

## ROME.

*THIS IS THE CAPITAL* of Italy, and once it was the capital of the world. It was a wicked city then, full of idols and cruelty—and it is a wicked city now. Here the Pope lives. He is the chief of all the priests of the Roman Catholic religion.

❖ ❖ ❖ ❖ ❖

## NAPLES.

*NAPLES IS MUCH MORE BEAUTIFUL* than Rome. It is built by the sea-side, where the land is in the shape of a half-moon. This is called a bay. Naples is a gay city. The people are always moving about and talking fast. The streets are full of carts and carriages laden with people,—some before, and some behind, and some underneath; for even poor people like to have a ride. In Rome the people are grave and silent, but in Naples they are merry and noisy. Which city should you like best?

**MOUNT VESUVIUS.**——This mountain is very near Naples. It is a terrible mountain, for fire comes out of a hole at the top. Very few people dare to look down the hole at the top. It is foolish to look down, for no one can tell when the hot boiling stuff called lava will burst forth.

# GERMANY.

Their peoples' agitation notwithstanding, the German and Prussian revolutions in 1848 lacked the strength and unity of the era's French and Italian revolts. Berlin was under siege by mid-November, but rebellions here and in other German capitals in led to a divided Frankfurt Assembly that called for unification with Austria. The Assembly failed in March 1849, after Prussia's King Frederick William IV declined to serve as the emperor. A treaty with Austria to maintain the German union was signed in 1850. Werner von Siemens invented the dial telegraph in 1846, and Richard Wagner produced the opera *Lohengrin* between 1846 and 1848. Robert Bunsen created the Bunsen burner in 1850; five years later, Karl Benz invented the gasoline automobile.

IF YOU WERE TRAVELLING through Germany you would see fine hills and great forests; but you would not see those pretty green fields and hedges all covered with May which are so pleasant in England. Where are the cows? They are in the stable. How strange it seems to keep the poor cow shut up in a stall! I am sure if you were a cow you would much sooner be an American cow feasting on the fresh grass than a German cow eating the bundles of weeds in a stable.

I cannot say the cottages are very pleasant. The lower room is the cow's stable. This would be well if the upper room was clean; but it is not. As the women are so much out of doors, they do not keep the house clean. There is a dresser with the shelves, beds with curtains, and a stove; but all is dirty and uncomfortable.

**FOOD.**——The Germans get up very early, and have breakfast at six or seven o'clock, but they are content with a cup of coffee, and some dry bread; and they usually drink a glass of cold water before they begin.

They do not often drink tea, nor do they know well how to make it. I have heard of a maid at an inn who by mistake boiled the tea.

**APPEARANCE.**——Many of the Germans are stout, tall, fine-looking men,—and no wonder, because they have plenty of good food, and hard work to make it agree with them. The women are fresh and fair, with round smiling faces, light hair, and blue eyes.

The ladies are very industrious, and wherever they go, they take their knitting. They are as fond of their knitting-needles as the gentlemen are of their pipes. The number of stockings they make would surprise you. How much better to knit than to smoke! When they are at home, the ladies spend a great deal of time in cooking; they also spin, and have a great deal of linen of their own spinning, locked up in their great chests. Can they do nothing but knit, and cook, and spin? Yes, they can play on the piano, and the harp, and sing very sweetly. But they are not fond of reading useful books. When they read, it is novels about people who have never lived. It would be better to read nothing than such books.

At Christmas time, the parents please their children by getting a little tree, and sticking lights all over it, and hanging sham fruit and little figures upon it, and on the table near it they lay presents. But very naughty children are not allowed to see the tree, or to have any presents.

**CHARACTER.**——You must have seen already, that the Germans are very kind, and pleasant in their families. They are affectionate. They are careful, and cautious. It would be well if they were more neat and clean, especially the poor people.

# *A U S T R I A .*

In 1848, revolts against the expansionist empire wrecked Bohemia, Hungary, and Italy, and by mid-March, Vienna was in open rebellion. Emperor Ferdinand fled the imperial palace in mid-May, followed by foreign minister Prince Klemens von Metternich's escape to London, but Austria's army crushed all revolts by 1851, and the nation's young constitution was abolished the next year. Despite its expansionist tendencies, Austria's empire continued to slow in the 1850s—its 1857 population of 37.3 million had grown by just two million over the previous fifteen years. In 1851, Wilhelm Steinitz won the first modern international chess tournament in London.

ONE PART OF GERMANY is called Austria. The Emperor who reigns over it has a great deal of power. Yet he is very kind, as you will think when I tell you, that on a certain day every week any poor person may come and make his complaints to him, as to a father.

◇　◇　◇　◇　◇

## VIENNA.

THERE ARE NO PEOPLE so fond of parties as the people of Vienna. Morning, noon, and evening, they are thinking of treats, and holidays, of music and dancing. They are fond also of eating nice things.

The streets are full of carriages, driving along very fast, and it is very hard to get out of their way, because there is no pavement to walk on. When the carriages are driving around a narrow corner, the frightened people sometimes jump upon the carriage, rather than be

run over by it; so that you may often see carriages with people cling-
ing to them before and behind.

The streets are kept very clean, yet there is a black stream in the
middle of the city which is very unpleasant, and makes the place unwholesome. A great many people have coughs in Vienna, because the
east wind blows very cold.

---

# HUNGARY.

The revolutionary spirit sweeping Europe took hold here in the late
1840s, when liberal parties tried to establish autonomy from the Hapsburg empire's rule. In 1848, Austria permitted Hungary to form its own
semi-autonomous government; King Ferdinand V abdicated in December, and his nephew Francis-Joseph assumed power as the king of
Hungary and emperor of Austria. Hungary declared complete independence in April 1849 but was crushed four months later by Austrian
and Russian troops, and Hapsburg rule was re-established in 1851. Between 1846 and 1855, Franz Liszt produced the *Hungarian Rhapsodies,*
nineteen works incorporating national dances and melodies.

HUNGARY IS A MUCH WARMER COUNTRY than Germany,
because there are high mountains which serve as a screen against the
north and east winds. Look at them. They are called the Carpathian
Mountains.

The Hungarians are a much wilder people than the Germans; they
are not industrious; they do not know how to make things; most of
them cannot read or write.

There are so many wolves in Hungary that the people often make a strong hedge of pricking thorns all round the village to keep them out. It is dangerous to walk about at night in lonely places.

**THE FOREST.**——If you were to travel in the forest of Bakony, you would see a great number of pigs feeding on the acorns under the trees. The men who take care of these pigs are called swine-herds. They have not such a pleasant employment as shepherds have. Who could like as well to take care of dirty, greedy, grunting pigs, as of clean, soft, bleating sheep?

These poor swine-herds know nothing, and many of them are robbers. They do not rob the poor, but sometimes they join together to rob rich lords in their castles. Very often they are caught and killed; but they are not ashamed of stealing; they think it a fine thing to be a brave robber. I advise you, if you go to Bakony forest, not to go too near the pigs, for they are very fierce. The swine-herds, when they please, can make their pigs attack men and tear them to pieces.

Almost everyone in Hungary is either very rich or very poor. The rich people have such magnificent castles, that there are none like them to be seen elsewhere. But the poor live in huts made of sticks, without even mud to keep out the cold air, and the rain; and some live like wild beasts in dens under ground, while their little children, neither washed, nor combed, nor clothed, play all day at the door in the midst of pigs, goats, dogs, hens, and ducks.

◇　◇　◇　◇　◇

## BUDA AND PESTH.

*HUNGARY HAS TWO CAPITALS,* and they are near each other. The broad river Danube rolls between them. But these cities are very unlike each other. Buda is built among hills covered with vines. Pesth is on flat ground, and has a great deal of trade with the ships up the river.

Buda is poor; Pesth is rich. Buda is old; Pesth is new (at least the greater part). Buda is full of gardens; Pesth of handsome buildings. Which should you like best? I am sorry to say the people at Buda and Pesth do not like each other; they are envious of one another.

---

# PRUSSIA.

The 1855 population of Prussia proper was 2,636,766, with some additional fifteen million living throughout the monarchy. Prussia's railway expanded by 84 percent—from 1787 miles to 2725 miles—in the decade after 1848, and its roads, considered miserable at the start of the century, were regarded as plentiful and excellent by the mid-1800s. Prussia's criminal law was codified and standardized throughout the monarchy in 1851.

PRUSSIA IS NOT a pretty country. It is full of sandy plains, and ugly bogs, and low fir-trees. Neither is it a healthy country. The east wind blows very sharp, and the ground is very damp. Yet in one respect it is a good country, for the religion is Protestant. There are also many good laws, and the poor people are taught to read. It is a pity there are so many soldiers.

FOOD.——The Prussians are not fond of eating, like the Austrians. They are content with bread and butter.

Though the Prussians are not fond of eating, they are too fond of drinking drams. They say they have no good beer or wine. That is true; but could they not find something better to drink than brandy, which makes their faces pale, hurts their health, and causes many quarrels?

✧ ✧ ✧ ✧ ✧

## BERLIN.

*THE CHIEF CITY OF PRUSSIA* is Berlin. It is built on a sandy plain. All at once you see a very handsome gate just before you; there is hardly one like it in all of Europe.

When you have passed through the gate, you enter a very fine street. It is the finest in Europe. There is an avenue down the middle of lime trees, and chestnut trees. The houses in this street belong to great lords. At the end of the street, which is nearly a mile long, there is a great square all of sand, without any grass. On one side is the king's palace.

Do you think you should like Berlin? I have not told you yet of the kennels, or ditches, which are found in every part, even near the king's palace, and which are so black and dirty, that the whole city is quite unpleasant in summer-time. I need not say that the black river, and the black kennels, are very bad for the health, and many more people die in Berlin than in London.

You will see soldiers at every step you take. They crowd the gin-shops. These are very handsome buildings, with looking-glasses on the walls, and beautiful lights hanging from the ceiling, and rows of bottles of all colours to tempt the foolish to buy.

I am sorry to say, that though Prussia is a Protestant country, the people do not keep the Sunday holy, but even go to the play in the evening.

✧ ✧ ✧ ✧ ✧

## POTSDAM.

*THOUGH BERLIN IS SO FLAT,* there is a place twenty miles off, that is very beautiful. Upon the hills are built many beautiful

— 63 —

palaces, which everybody may see. In one of the palaces there is a room where a very wicked Frenchman once lived. His name was Voltaire. Voltaire has written a great many books, which have taught people to despise God and to serve Satan.

**CHARACTER.**——The Prussians are like the Germans; and, indeed, they are Germans, for most of Prussia is called Germany. But they are more lively, and not so slow or so steady. They are not as fond of company, or of feasting, as the Austrians. Every one smokes, both rich and poor, and even boys begin very early to imitate their fathers in this idle, disagreeable habit. The gentlemen and ladies are very polite, and fond of paying compliments; but the shopkeepers are uncivil, and do not seem to like to take the trouble of showing their goods.

*YOU MAY GO A GREAT WAY IN POLAND*
*WITHOUT SEEING ANYTHING PRETTY.*

# *POLAND*.

Revolution was not new to Poland by the late 1840s; Russia had already crushed an 1830 revolt, turning Poland into a province under the czar. Polish arts and literature were suppressed throughout the 1830s and 1840s; the media were censored heavily, and a Russian police/espionage system was established. The Republic of Kraków revolted in mid-November 1846, declaring independence and its own annexation to Austria; Russia put down the revolution the following year. At the end of the 1850s, nearly three quarters of the Kingdom of Poland's 4.8 million people were Roman Catholic, and 600,000 were Jewish.

WHAT A CHANGE IT IS to go from Prussia into a country that joins it! It is the people that are so different. In Prussia the children are neatly dressed and go to school, but in Poland they are ragged and dirty, and little beggars run after the carriages calling out, "Kleba, kleba!" which means "Bread, bread!"

**TO WHOM POLAND BELONGS.**——Poor Poland has no king of her own. She has been torn to pieces by three great countries—Austria, Russia, and Prussia. They have divided Poland between them. This was very wrong.

**COTTAGES.**——These are miserable places, made only of trunks of trees piled one upon another, with a little hole cut out in the side to let in light and to let out smoke. There is no bed,—but straw laid upon some boards.

**COUNTRY.**——You may go a great way without seeing anything pretty. Poland is a plain of sand. When the wind blows hard, the sand gets into your eyes and mouth. Sometimes the ground is soft, and the carriage can hardly get along—it is passing over a marsh.

**FOOD.**——The poor can get milk, because they have cows. But their food is not very good. Potatoes and cabbages, and barley-gruel—they are the chief food. The drink is beer and spirits. The Poles are a great deal too fond of spirits.

**THE JEWS.**——All children who have read the Bible, know that the Jews were once called Israelites, and that they once lived in the land of Canaan. Where do they live now? In all lands; but more Jews live in Poland than in any other country. You might know them in a moment by their long black muslin gowns, and their long black shining beards. In 1847 the Emperor of Russia forbid the Jews to wear their own dress any more, and this cruel law cost the Jews many tears. They have eyes like the hawk and noses like its beak. They are fine-looking men—such as you might imagine David and Solomon were.

The rich Jewesses wear bright turbans, adorned with diamonds and rubies. But all the Jews are not rich. Some are miserably poor.

The Jews are not idle like the Poles, but try in every way to get money. It is they who keep all the inns—and wretched inns they are, because the Jews are very dirty. Go in at that low covered doorway, taking care not to hit your head (unless you are only a little boy or girl). The floor has no carpet, nor even boards—no—nor bricks—it is the bare earth. There are boards in one corner with some straw on them. Would you rather sleep there or in that little dark room beyond? Look in; it is full of dirty beds, and children of all sizes. In that dark room the old Jew, who has been selling beer all day, often sits up at night and lights his lamp to read his old books.

The Jews are very troublesome in Poland. They follow travellers about, offering to help them, and will not go away when they are told. The Poles speak very rudely to the Jews, and think themselves much better; but the Jews bear rudeness with great patience, because they are accustomed to be ill-treated.

**CHARACTER.**——The Poles used to be called the "Proud Poles."

The nobles treated the poor very cruelly. A lord often took away a poor man's cow, and the poor man in return cut down the lord's tree. All the Poles are either great lords or poor people. It is the Jews or the Germans who buy and sell. The gentlemen in Poland are too proud to work.

The Poles love talking, and they speak so loud they almost scream; and they are proud of this, and say that the Germans are dumb.

<hr />

# *HOLLAND*.

Between 1815 and 1830, the Kingdom of the Netherlands incorporated Holland, Belgium, and Luxembourg under King William I; Belgium broke away in 1830. The end of the 1840s saw a rapid succession of rulers: William I's restless subjects forced him to abdicate in 1848, and his son, William II, who immediately granted a new constitution, died the following March, yielding the throne to William III. The predominant Dutch industry was foreign trade, and the country's great prosperity was bolstered by its rule over eighteen million colonial subjects from Surinam to Sumatra. By 1863, when the Dutch abolished slavery, the Netherlands supported 226 publications and universities at Leyden, Utrecht, and Groningen; each community was required to establish at least one public elementary school.

THERE IS NO COUNTRY in the world so damp as Holland. There is so much water that every place is wet; indeed, people could not live there at all if it were not for the pains they take to make it a little more dry. Even the cows are often made sick by the damp.

**CHARACTER.**——There is no people in Europe as clean as the Dutch. If they did not rub and scrub a good deal, the damp would cover all their brass pans with rust.

The poor children at school are much cleaner than English children.

The Dutch are very industrious. The king will not allow big boys to stand idle in the streets. The policemen take up idle ragged boys, and send them into the country to drain the marshy grounds; so there are very few thieves, and hardly any beggars.

The Dutch children do not make as much noise at school as our children do. You hear no noise outside the school-house, and when playtime comes the scholars go out quietly. They cannot help making some noise with their feet, as they wear wooden shoes,—and wooden shoes, I think, they must need to keep them out of the wet.

**RELIGION.**——Are you not already sure that there is a good religion in this country? The Protestant is the religion.

The Dutch do not take their pleasure on Sundays as the Germans do, though they do not rest as much as they ought. They keep the Sabbath in much the same manner as in England.

❖   ❖   ❖   ❖   ❖

## AMSTERDAM.

*THIS IS THE CAPITAL* of Holland. There is no city in which there is so much danger of being drowned, for it is full of canals.

There are a great many rich people in Amsterdam, and the way they get rich is by sending ships laden with goods to other countries, and bringing them back full of other things, and selling them to all who will buy.

But there is so much water in Amsterdam, there is very little water fit to drink, so that the people either buy water of men who bring water-carts, or they drink rain-water. Still the water is very useful for keeping the city clean. The servant girls may be seen in the morning in their wooden-shoes, pouring buckets in the street, and dashing water against the sides of the houses.

---

# BELGIUM.

Following its declaration of independence from the Dutch in 1830, Belgium adopted a liberal constitution recognizing freedom of religion and the press. 1848's pan-European tensions were relatively mild in Belgium, where the military defeated a conspiracy to overthrow King Leopold I, who promised to abdicate if the people wished and who ruled until his 1865 death. In March 1848, with much of Europe in revolt, Belgium averted a financial panic by suspending cash payments and issuing public credit. Already a leader in railway transportation, Belgium introduced its first telegraph, between Brussels and Antwerp, in 1849. The nation's population in 1851—decades before Leopold II would raid the Congo—was 4.4 million.

*I SHALL NOT SAY MUCH* about Belgium, because it is so like the countries on each side. The people are in some things like the Dutch; they are steady, sober, and industrious; but in some things they are like the French, they are quick and lively. They speak the French language, though some of the people speak a language of their own, called Flemish; but the names of the trades over the shops, and the names of the streets are written in French.

There are a great many neat little farm-houses among the fields.

Each farm is not larger than a good-sized field, that is, about six acres; yet on this small piece of land the whole family live comfortably. They must then be industrious. Yes, not one in the family is idle.

The farmer works very hard, for often he has no plough, and no cart, and no horse. Therefore he digs his land with his spade, and wheels along his barrow full of hay. This is slow work, but it is the only way these poor people can manage. They live on common food.

Do you not hope that these industrious, honest people, love to read their Bibles in their pleasant cottages? Alas! they worship idols. They are Roman Catholics.

✧  ✧  ✧  ✧  ✧

## BRUSSELS.

*THIS IS THE CHIEF CITY* of Belgium. It is built on the sunny side of a hill, and is a very handsome town.

There is a fountain in Brussels and a brass image of a boy near it. This brass image is called "The Mannekin." This image has a servant to wait upon it and to dress it up very fine on holidays. Many kings have given presents to the Mannekin. One gave him a soldier's dress. You are ready to laugh at the people of Brussels, and to call them very silly; but they are sensible in many things, only they do not understand the Scriptures, and so they honour images.

# S W I T Z E R L A N D .

The reformist movements of the 1830s and 1840s put this mountainous country in turmoil. A peasant mob overturned the government in Zürich in 1839, the Protestant Diet overthrew Lucerne's Jesuit rulers in a brief civil war in 1847, and the country adopted a new democratic constitution in 1848. The country's chief industries were diverse: silk-stuffs and cottons in Zurich, leather and tobacco in Basel, watches and jewelry in Geneva. By 1860, Switzerland had 188 political journals, forty daily papers, five universities, and no standing army (although every citizen was obliged to serve).

THERE IS NO COUNTRY in Europe as beautiful as Switzerland; it is the land of high mountains, and deep valleys, and bubbling streams, and roaring waterfalls. People come from all countries to see Switzerland. But if you are afraid of going up steep paths, you had better not go there, for you would have to travel in high places by the side of terrible precipices.

Some travellers have fallen over the precipices, and some have sunk into the cracks of the snow, because they had nobody to show them the way. Some have been frozen in the snow, and would have died had they not been found by the good dogs sent out by the monks of St. Bernard.

In some places the Swiss children make toys to sell. It must be pleasant to see these industrious children earning bread for themselves and their poor parents.

But there are a great many idle little beggars who run after the travellers as they go slowly up the mountains. These are dirty little creatures, with hands unwashed and hair uncombed.

As you pass through the villages, you will often see poor children sitting by the wayside with their heads bent down, their eyes rolling, and their mouths open. What is the matter with these unhappy creatures? They are idiots. They have hardly any sense. Yet their parents love them even more than their other children. Do not mock or despise them, for they have immortal souls, and some of them can pray to God, though they cannot work or read.

**RELIGION.**——There is not one king over all Switzerland. No, there are a great many people who rule over it, and some rule over one part, and some over another. Neither is there one sort of *character*. The Mountaineers are simple, honest creatures, but those who live in the valleys are more cunning and clever. Neither is there one *religion;* in some parts it is the Roman Catholic, in others the Protestant.

*EVEN THE POOR MEN AMONG THE MOUNTAINS*
*GO DOWN TO THE PUBLIC-HOUSE*
*ON SUNDAY EVENING, AND DRINK WINE.*

The Protestants follow one of the bad customs of the Roman Catholics; they amuse themselves on Sunday. Even the poor men among the mountains go down to the public-house on Sunday evening, and drink wine; and though they do not get drunk, they ought not to be there.

**MOUNTAINS.**——When people go to Switzerland for the first time, they often think, "How happy should I be to live in a cottage here, to look down upon those sweet lakes, to hear that grand waterfall, and to gaze upon the snowy peaks of those high mountains!" But very often a great lump of snow as big as a house, rolls down the side of a mountain, and making a noise as loud as thunder, crushes a cottage that lies on the side! O, what a terrible disaster! But I am going to tell you of a worse.

It was on the 2d of September, 1806, about five o'clock in the afternoon, that the earth began to slide. Very slowly it went at first. A young man felt the ground giving way, and called out to an old man to come away; but the old man, who was smoking his pipe by his door, said, "I have time to fill my pipe once more," and he went back, and the house fell upon him, and killed him, but the young man running as fast as he could, though he often fell down, escaped.

## *D E N M A R K .*

The Slesvig and Holstein duchies, at the south of the Danish kingdom, tried to shake off Denmark's rule and join Germany in 1848. Under pressure from his subjects, King Frederik VII assented in 1849 to adopting a democratic constitution with a legislature, the bicameral

Rigsdag, but the question of the monarchy's line of succession continued to anger the duchies. Denmark put down the rebellion in July 1850
but ultimately ceded the territories to Germany.

*I* SHALL TELL YOU very little about Denmark, because it is so
much like England.

The language is a good deal like English. In old times, the Danes
used to go often over to England, and no doubt the English learned
some of their words. The Danes are also like the Dutch, a steady,
quiet people, but they are not such a busy, money-getting nation.

Denmark is flat, but not nearly as flat as Holland, nor as damp, nor
as ugly.

◇ ◇ ◇ ◇ ◇

## COPENHAGEN.

*THIS IS THE CAPITAL.* There is not so regular and handsome a
town in all Europe; but as the ground is flat, it cannot be as beautiful
as Edinburgh.

If you like a quiet city, you would like Copenhagen. It is so still
and so silent, that you might almost think there was nobody in it.

**CHARACTER.**——The Danes possess a great many good qualities,
but they are too fond of feasting and amusements. They are not
drunken, like most northern nations. A traveller who spent some
months in Denmark said when he left it, "I never saw in this land a
cripple, or a beggar, or a drunken person, either in the day or night."
This could not be said by a traveller through England.

# *I C E L A N D .*

The volcanic North Atlantic island was Danish property in the mid-nineteenth century. The Althing, the nine-hundred-year-old national parliament, was suspended in 1800 and re-established in 1843. Between 1840 and 1855, the country's tiny population grew by more than seven thousand to roughly sixty-five thousand, some 1,350 of whom lived in Reykjavik. The town then boasted an observatory, three newspapers, and a public library with eight thousand volumes. Iceland's major exports included wool, feathers, skins, and fish oil; its 1855 imports amounted to 40,000 barrels of Danish grain, 448,000 quarts of liquor and 109,000 pounds of tobacco.

WHAT SORT OF COUNTRY IS THIS? Its name just suits it. The first person who found Iceland called it Snow-land, because he could see nothing but snow; but the next person called it Iceland, because of the large heaps of ice floating near the shores.

Yet you will be surprised to hear that there is more hot water in Iceland than in any other country. What is the reason? There is fire underground, which makes the water hot. There are many hollow places in the ground, like basins, full of hot water. You must take care not to fall into one of these basins, for your poor little legs would be scalded. Some water is only just warm, and you could bathe there. Sometimes the Icelanders do bathe in the warm basins—not as often as they should, for they are a dirty people—even their hands are so dirty that you would not like them to touch you or to help you off with your things.

Have you heard of the great mountain Hecla? It is a burning mountain. Sometimes the hot lava pours down on all the country round, and kills every one who cannot get out of the way quickly enough. So you see Iceland is not a very safe island to dwell in.

**FOOD.**——Iceland is so cold that very few plants will grow in it. Corn will not grow, except a little rye and a little barley—only a very, very little. How then can there be bread? There is very little. The poor people are obliged to do without it. They can get plenty of fish, and they dry it and eat it instead of bread. There is no fruit at all.

**HOUSES.**——There are no houses in the middle of Iceland; all the people live near the sea, that they may get fish.

There is only one town in all Iceland, and we should call it a small village. Its name is Reikiavik, and it is built by the sea-shore.

In the country, as you travel along, you will often see a farm-house, with a church, and a few huts near. The farm-house looks neat outside; but it is very low, and it has only two windows in front. The doors are painted red.

If you go into the house, you will soon wish to run out again—it is so dark and dirty. If you grope along the dark passage, you will come to a room at the end full of beds, and full of litter. The people heap wooden dishes, spinning-wheels, and old clothes in confusion upon the beds; and they never dust the furniture, nor scrub, nor even sweep the rooms. The little windows in the roof, not bigger than your hand, will not open. The house is never aired. What an unpleasant place!

**CHURCHES.**——It is pleasant to see so many little churches in the is-land. The religion of Iceland is the Protestant.

It is a pity the churches are not kept cleaner and neater. The farmer often turns the church into a lumber-room; sometimes there are so many boxes piled up in it, that the minister's face is almost hid. The farmer keeps his best clothes there, if he likes, and what is much worse, he lays by his dried fish there, and this fish gives the place a very unpleasant smell; and as the windows will not open, I think it would almost make you sick to go to church in Iceland.

**GOVERNMENT.**——Iceland has no king of her own, though she once had. She belongs to Denmark. The king of Denmark appoints a man to rule over Iceland. He is called the governor. The Danes are more like gentlemen than the Icelanders, but they are not as sober and steady. A great many Danes live in Reikiavik, and they have made the place much worse than it used to be. They set the example of drinking too much wine and brandy.

**CHARACTER.**——There are very few people as harmless and quiet as the Icelanders. They are dull and slow, but they are honest and true. They are fond and working and reading, and not fond of riot and folly.

They are never idle when they can help it. It is a pity they do not spend a little of their time in keeping their houses and themselves sweet and clean.

# S I C I L Y.

This island dependency of the Kingdom of Naples, its partner of the Two Sicilies, proudly hosted the very first European revolt of 1848. After rebels occupied Palermo in early January, they proclaimed Sicily's independence in April, announcing an intention to join a future Italian federation. Naples, under Austrian rule, crushed the rebellion in May 1849. By the early 1860s, Sicily was exporting more than five million gallons of wine annually to England, America, and India.

*THIS COUNTRY IS AN ISLAND.* Iceland also is an island, but how very different these two islands are!

Which should you think was the pleasanter country? Sicily, a great deal. Iceland is the coldest country in Europe, and Sicily the warmest (except, perhaps, for some little islands, too small to be considered countries).

How different are the plants in Sicily from those in Iceland! In Iceland, wheat will not grow at all, while in Sicily there is the finest grain. There are no fruit-trees in Iceland, but in Sicily you may buy twenty oranges for a penny.

But it is the people who are so very different in Iceland and Sicily. The Icelanders are a gentle, quiet, honest race, while the Sicilians are fierce, violent, and cruel. In the prison in Iceland, there are sometimes scarcely any thieves, while in Sicily the robbers are so bold, and so many, that it is a hard matter to catch them.

Poor people, who cannot keep guards to defend them, are quite frightened to go along the paths. Sometimes, as men are cutting stones by the wayside, a band of robbers will burst out, beat them well, and then leave them tied to trees, while they run off with their tools.

Almost every poor person in Sicily begs. How different it is in Iceland, where even poor people offer a draught of milk to the stranger!

**MOUNT ETNA.**——There is a burning mountain in Sicily, and a much larger one than Hecla.

Etna is a very tall mountain. Though only two miles high, yet you must travel more than twenty miles to get to the top. What do you see at the top? A great deep black hole, always smoking, and grumbling. Take care, do not stay too long, lest the mountain should throw out its boiling contents.

**DRESS.**——The gentlemen and ladies dress as they do in England. The poor men wear a loose cotton shirt, and drawers, with a red silk sash, and a brown or red woollen cap on their heads, while their feet are bare. They throw over all a large brown cloak, with a hood covering their heads. There are many murderers, who have need of a hood to hide their faces. Often there is a sharp dagger under the cloak.

❖  ❖  ❖  ❖  ❖

MESSINA.

*THIS IS THE PORT* by which people enter from Italy. It looks beautiful from the sea, with its white houses, and red roofs, and its high hills behind, clothed with vines and olives; but when you come near, you find narrow, dirty, ill-paved streets.

---

# *SWEDEN.*

The predominantly Lutheran Sweden, a constitutional democracy, suffered low grain yields and a growing population that began emigrating to North America in the late 1860s. King Oscar I, crowned in 1844, ruled over not only Sweden but also its resentful neighbor, Norway, annexed in an 1818 wartime treaty. The chief mid-nineteenth-century industries were agriculture, mining, and shipbuilding. Stockholm was the site of a violent outbreak against the Jews in early September 1852. The country adopted the decimal system in 1858.

*THERE IS A LARGE PIECE OF LAND* in the north that seems like the arm of Europe, as Italy looks like the leg. This arm is divided into two countries—Norway and Sweden. A long chain of mountains runs between them.

Both these countries are very cold; but in many respects they are very different, as you will see.

**FOOD.**——The Swedes have a curious way of dressing their meat. In England meat is boiled or roasted, but in Sweden meat is often only smoked. You would not like smoked salmon or smoked rein-deer flesh. But how should you like rough salmon? It is salmon not cooked at all. Yet the Swedes eat it often, mixing with it vinegar and pepper. Milk soup is another dish, and beer soup is another.

Even poor people eat five meals a day.

There is a bad custom of eating some food at a side-table, before sitting down to dinner: this is called getting an appetite for dinner, but I should think it was taking it away.

There is a much worse custom, of drinking a glass of spirits before meals three times a day. This habit is very bad for the health, and shortens the life.

**CHARACTER.**——Almost every one can read. In every little town there is a bookseller's shop, and sometimes there are more booksellers than butchers. It is never so in America, as you will see if you observe.

You are ready to think the Swedes are a wise and good people. Not so. There is no country in Europe where so many people are put in prison.

I do not mean to say that there are as many robbers in Sweden as in Sicily; there the robbers are seldom punished at all: in Sweden they are punished; but yet the rest of the people go on stealing. Travellers think the Swedes honest, because they do not steal their trunks; but I suppose they know they should be found out if they did, for the king has a great number of men watching to take up thieves. The Swedes swear also in a dreadful manner, the gentlemen as well as the poor people. They get drunk also very often.

The great people in Sweden set a bad example to the poor. There are many lords and ladies who spend all their time in dressing, and dancing, and singing foolish songs. The shopkeepers also neglect their business and waste their time.

The Swedes are very polite. Even the beggars will show their gratitude by kissing your sleeve or the skirt of your coat. But what is politeness compared to truth and honesty!

COTTAGES.——In the south of Sweden the cottages are uncomfortable. They are so small, that, to make more room, the beds are placed one above another, and you must climb up to the top bed, and when there, take care not to fall out. As you go along the road you will observe broken windows, unswept yards, torn thatch. It seems as if the people were idle, and cared not for their houses. But in the north there are many pretty neat villages—where all the cottage windows are furnished with muslin blinds and are adorned with gay flower-pots.

The Swedes do not care as much for comforts, as for ornaments. They have fine looking-glasses, and sofas, and chandeliers, and pictures, but they often do without basins, jugs, chests of drawers, curtains, and other useful furniture. Nothing useful is well done in Sweden. The carpenters and the blacksmiths are very clumsy in their work, but the musicians play beautifully, and the sculptors make fine statues.

---

# *N O R WA Y.*

The Norwegians, naturally, disputed and resented their 1818 annexation by the next-door neighbors. Still, King Oscar I's ascension in 1844 ushered in a peaceable period, as he instituted enlightened press reforms and abolished the poor tax. Norway's support of Denmark in the Slesvig-Holstein war in 1848 bloated the country's previously svelte national debt. In the mid-nineteenth century, only 11 percent of Norwegians lived in cities. The most common language was Danish, although attempts were underway to organize various regional dialects into more widely spoken Norwegian tongues. All Christians, even non-Lutherans, enjoyed religious freedom; Jews, however, were not tolerated.

**THE COUNTRY.**——Is there a more beautiful country in Europe than Norway? Switzerland is more beautiful, but Norway is the grandest country in Europe. There are mountains, waterfalls, and lakes, with such forests as are seen nowhere else.

**PEOPLE.**——What sort of people live in this wild country?

They are called Norwegians. The men are tall and strong; the women are handsome. They are a simple people—kind and good-natured, and particularly honest. In summer nights, which are quite light and very hot, the people leave their doors open, and no thief comes in, not even in the towns. Bars and bolts are of no use in Norway.

The greatest fault of the Norwegians is drunkenness. They are too fond of a spirit called finkel—something like gin, only it is made from potatoes. On every little farm there is a machine, called a still, for making it. O who can say how much mischief is done by that still!

The poor are ignorant, and not fond of reading, though they can read. They are not like the Icelanders, who drink little and read much.

**HOUSES.**——Most things in Norway are made of wood, because it is so plentiful. The wooden houses are painted—white, or green, or yellow; but they are not as pretty as the cottages in Switzerland.

The inns are generally very wretched. There is only one room for strangers, with two wooden cribs in it, a straw mattress, or else hay, coarse sheets, and a sheepskin or cowskin for a counterpane. The cups and plates are very few.

**FOOD.**——People who are dainty must not come to Norway. Barley-cakes as thin and round as plates, or rye-bread, with some coffee, may easily be had. There is also the best butter in the world. But the rivers are full of fish. This is the chief food. One traveller wondered what made his room so unpleasant, and at last he found there was a great well full of fish in the floor, just covered over.

There are often famines, and then saw-dust is mixed with the bread, and the poor cows are fed on a sort of paste made up of rubbish of various sorts.

**RELIGION.**—It is the Protestant. Yet if you were to enter a church you would fear that it was Roman Catholic, because at one end there is an altar with small images upon it of the Virgin and of the saints. Yet you would soon find out that there is a better religion than the Roman Catholic, for the prayers are not said in Latin, nor are images worshipped.

After service the Sabbath is not kept holy. There is dancing, and drinking, and merry-making. No wonder therefore that most people are very ignorant.

# *T U R K E Y.*

A series of wars against Europe's stronger nations loosened the Ottoman Empire's grip on much of the Mediterranean and Middle East throughout the nineteenth century—although the Ottoman Empire's British- and French-assisted defeat of Russia in the 1853–1856 Crimean War broke the czar's dominance over the Balkans and the Black Sea for a couple of decades. A Turkish-born Englishman founded the country's most important political newspaper, *Djeridei Havadis,* in 1843. A new education system, introduced in 1847, began establishing elementary schools across the country. In 1849, Turkey suffered a brief trade embargo when it refused to surrender Hungarian and Polish refugees who had fled from Austrian and Russian rule.

*THIS LAND IS VERY DIFFERENT* from all the other countries in Europe—and this is the reason: it has a different religion. All the other countries are called Christian, but Turkey is a Mahomedan country. What is that?

Once there was a man named Mahomet, who told people he was a prophet sent from God; but he was a false prophet, and a wicked man. He wrote a book called the Koran, and filled it with foolish stories, and absurd laws, and horrible lies.

The places where the Turks worship are called mosques. They are very much like churches, only there are no seats, but carpets are spread on the marble floor.

❖ ❖ ❖ ❖ ❖

## CONSTANTINOPLE.

*THE CHIEF TOWN IN TURKEY* is built by the sea. Like many other towns it looks beautiful at a distance, but turns out, when you arrive there, to be very unpleasant. The golden tops of the mosques peeping and sparkling among the tall cypress trees, and the gardens sloping down to the water's edge, make it appear lovely; but the narrow dirty streets disgust the stranger who walks in them.

**THE GRAND SEIGNOR.**—The king of Turkey is called the Sultan, or the Grand Seignor. He has a palace by the water-side where his wives live. They are all slaves brought from distant parts, and chosen for their beauty.

The Grand Seignor does what he pleases. He orders any one who offends him to be killed.

It is one of the wicked customs of this dark land to murder the boy-babies of the king's brothers. The reason is lest they are grown up any of them should try to make himself Grand Seignor.

**ANIMALS.**——If you lived in Turkey you would not be fond of dogs. There are a number of hungry dogs roaming about Constantinople, and eating up all the dead things or offal, lying in the streets. I will tell you an anecdote about them.

An English lady was walking one morning with her little niece in a burial-ground in Constantinople, amongst the shady trees and beds of flowers;——when suddenly she saw troops of hungry dogs approaching her from every quarter. There they were on every side, with their sharp teeth and glaring eyes, and noses snuffing the air, as if they smelt something very nice. The lady knew not what to do. She tried to reach the gate, dragging the child after her, while the dogs followed—howling and raging, and even daring to take her dress between their teeth. At last she came close to the door; then, flinging the bread as far as she could from her, she rushed through and escaped by a narrow path to the inn.

At night such troops of fierce dogs walk about the streets that people carry in their hands whips to defend themselves.

**CHARACTER OF THE TURKS.**——They are so grave that they look wise. But how can lazy people be really wise? They like to spend their time in eating opium, sipping coffee, and sitting still. They are so lazy that, though the land is very fruitful, they do not sow grain enough for their own bread, but send for grain to other countries. They read scarcely anything but the Koran, which they learn by heart. Yet in one respect they are to be praised. It is this. They bear troubles well.

# GREECE.

The 1829 revolt against Turkish rule, assisted by Britain, Russia, and France, gave Greece a teenage Bavarian king, Otho I, three years later; in 1843, he was forced by a bloodless coup to adopt a constitution that diminished Bavarian authority. Britain and France blockaded the harbor at Piræus in an 1850 trade dispute and later helped suppress Greece's rebellion against the Ottoman Empire during the Crimean War. In 1852, the country was split into ten provinces; the king chose all senators, who earned five hundred drachmas a month. By 1863, Greece boasted five thousand mercantile ships but fewer than one hundred miles of navigable road "fit for a donkey cart."

**COUNTRY.**——Greece is one of the lovely countries—*perhaps* it is the *most* beautiful—but we cannot be certain, for some people would say Switzerland.

But there is one beauty in Greece which is not to be found in Switzerland; this is—very fine old ruins, or remains of beautiful buildings.

What is the reason? When the other countries of Europe were filled with savages, then Greece was filled with clever men.

**ROBBERS.**——Once it was quite dangerous to go about in the mountains, so many murders were committed there. But lately a great deal of pains have been taken to frighten the robbers. The king rewards every poor man who brings a robber's head in his hand.

**CHILDREN.**——The Greeks do not know how to bring up their children. I will relate an anecdote of one spoiled child.

An English lady was in a ship not far from Athens. When it grew dark she went down into the cabin. There she saw a Greek lady lying on the floor, twisting her hands in her long hair, weeping, and lamenting aloud, and crying out, "If the ship do not return to Athens immediately, I do not know what I shall do!" "What is the matter?" asked the English lady. "Oh," said she, "I have a little daughter of seven years old, and she wishes to go home; and when we told her she could not, she began to scream violently, and is still screaming so loud that I fear she will go into fits."

The English lady tried to quiet the naughty child by giving her cakes and sugar-plums. This plan succeeded. If the child had not been spoiled ever since she was a baby, she would not have been so wilful and passionate at seven years old.

**CHARACTER.**—The Greeks are very unlike the Turks. They are lively and warm in their manners, and fond of talking. They love singing, though they sing badly. They delight in dancing and merriment. They give way to all their feelings, crying one moment and laughing another. They do not bear their troubles well; when they are unhappy, they scream like babies.

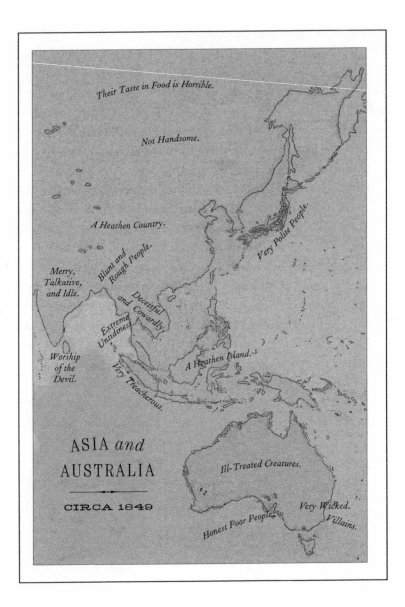

## PART II

# THE
# DRUNKEST
# LABOURERS
# IN
# ASIA;

SELECTIONS FROM

*Far Off: Asia and Australia Described,*

with Anecdotes and
Numerous Illustrations,

1852.

# THE HOLY LAND.

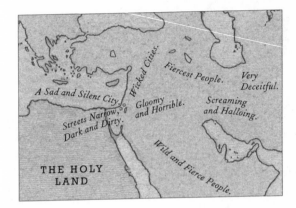

A Sad and Silent City.

Wicked Cities.

Fiercest People.

Very Deceitful.

Streets Narrow, Dark and Dirty.

Gloomy and Horrible.

Screaming and Halloing.

Wild and Fierce People.

THE HOLY LAND

In the mid-nineteenth century, the Ottoman Empire ruled over what was variously known as Palestine, Canaan, and the Land of Israel—home to diverse communities of Syrians, Mohammedans, Maronites, Druses, Christians, Turks, and Jews. In 1838 the British established a consulate in Jerusalem, Palestine's Jewish capital: a city of narrow, unpaved streets and gloomy houses, with twenty-five thousand inhabitants living in the Jewish, Armenian, Mohammedan, and Christian quarters. Jerusalem's revenue came largely from the ten thousand pilgrims who visited annually and bought locally made beads, crucifixes, and tablets of mother-of-pearl. Olives and figs were produced throughout the region, as well as in Lebanon and Syria; the best local wine was stomped at Hebron and Bethlehem.

OF ALL THE COUNTRIES in the world which would you rather see?

Would it not be the land where Jesus lived?

What is the land where He lived? Canaan was once its name: but now Palestine, or the Holy Land.

What place in the Holy Land do you wish most to visit?

I will take you first to Bethlehem.

❖ ❖ ❖ ❖ ❖

## BETHLEHEM.

A *GOOD MINISTER* visited this place, accompanied by a train of servants, and camels, and asses.

Bethlehem is on a steep hill, and a white road of chalk leads up to the gate. The traveller found the streets narrow, dark, and dirty. He lodged in a convent kept by Spanish monks. He was shown into a large room with carpets and cushions on the floor. There he was to sleep.

The next day, as the traveller was ready to mount his camel, the people of Bethlehem came with little articles which they had made. But he would not buy them, because they were images of the Virgin Mary and her holy child, and little white crosses of mother-o'-pearl. They were very pretty: but they were idols, and God hates idols.

❖ ❖ ❖ ❖ ❖

## JERUSALEM.

THE *CHILDREN OF JERUSALEM* once loved the Lord, and sung His praises in the temple.

Which is the place where the temple stood?

It is the Mount Moriah. There is a splendid building now on that Mount.

Is it the temple? Oh, no, that was burned many hundreds of years ago. It is the Mosque of Omar; it is the most magnificent mosque in all the world. How sad to think that Mahomedans should worship now in the very spot where once the Son of God taught the people.

But there is a place still dearer to our hearts than Mount Moriah. It is Calvary. There is a church on Calvary: but such a church! a church full of images and crosses. Roman Catholics worship there—and Greeks too: and they often fight in it, for they hate one another, and have fierce quarrels.

On Good Friday the monks carry all round the church an image of the Saviour as large as life, and they fasten it upon a cross, and take it down again, and put in the sepulchre, and they take it out again on Easter Sunday. How foolish and how wrong are these customs?

But there is another place—very sad but very sweet—where you must come. Go down that valley—cross that small stream—(there is a narrow bridge)—see those low stone walls—enter: it is the Garden of Gethsemane. Eight aged olive-trees are still standing there; but Jesus comes there no more with His beloved disciples.

And what kind of a city is Jerusalem?

It is a sad and silent city. The houses are dark and dirty, the streets are narrow, and the pavement rough. There are a great many very old Jews there. Jews come from all countries when they are old to Jerusalem, that they may die and be buried there. Their reason is that they think that all Jews who are buried in their real burial-ground at Jerusalem will be raised *first* at the last day, and will be happy for ever. Most of the old Jews are very poor: though money is sent to them every year from the Jews in Europe.

There are also a great many sick Jews in Jerusalem, because it is such an unhealthy place. The water in the wells and pools gets very bad in summer, and gives the ague and even the plague.

❖ ❖ ❖ ❖ ❖

## THE DEAD SEA.

*THE MOST GLOOMY AND HORRIBLE PLACE* in the Holy Land is the Dead Sea. In that place there once stood four wicked cities, and God destroyed them with fire and brimstone.

You have heard of Sodom and Gomorrah.

A clergyman who went to visit the Dead Sea rode on horseback, and was accompanied by men to guard him on the way, as there are robbers hid among the rocks.

He went next to look at the river Jordan. How different a place from the dreary, desolate Dead Sea! There is a place where the Roman Catholics bathe, and another where the Greeks bathe every year: they would not on any account bathe in the same part, because they disagree so much.

There is much to make the traveller sad as he wanders about the Holy Land.

That land was once *fruitful*, but now it is barren. It is not surprising that no one plants and sows in the fields, because the Turks would take away the harvest.

Once it was a *peaceful* land, but now there are so many enemies that every man carries a gun to defend himself.

Once it was a *holy* land, but now Mahomet is honoured, and not the God of Israel.

When shall it again be fruitful, and peaceful, and holy? When the Jews shall repent of their sins and turn to the Lord.

# ARABIA.

In the early nineteenth century, Arabia was disputed territory, seized periodically by Egypt and the Ottoman Empire even as it struggled for its own independence. The Saud family regained control over the country within a few years of an Egyptian conquest in 1819; the Saudi emir Faysal I ibn Turki, captured in 1838 and imprisoned in Cairo, escaped five years later and led Arabia until 1865. The 1854 *Encyclopædia Americana* noted that the Arabs, traditionally a nomadic society, had developed a passionate love of liberty and justice, and that their schools taught astronomy, history, poetry, pharmacology, and "philosophy, so called." "They practise robbery," the editors allowed, "but never at the expense of the laws of hospitality."

*THIS IS THE LAND* in which the Israelites wandered for forty years. You have heard what a dry, dreary, desert place the wilderness was. There is still a wilderness in Arabia; and there are still wanderers in it; not Israelites, but Arabs. These men live in tents, and go from place to place with their large flocks of sheep and goats.

And what sort of people are the Arabs?

Wild and fierce people.

Travellers are afraid of passing through Arabia, lest the Arabs should rob and murder them; and no one has ever been able to conquer the Arabs. The Arabs are very proud, and will not bear the least affront. The Arabs are so unforgiving and revengeful that they will seek to kill a man year after year.

**ARAB CUSTOMS.**——The Arabs sit on the ground, resting on their heels, and for tables they have low stools. A large dish of rice and minced mutton is placed on the table, and immediately every hand is thrust into it; and in a moment it is empty. They eat very fast, and each retires from dinner as soon as he likes, without waiting for the rest. After dinner they drink water, and a small cup of coffee without milk or sugar. Then they smoke for many hours.

The Arabs do not indulge in eating or drinking too much, and this is one of the best parts of their character.

## THE THREE EVILS OF ARABIA.

*THE FIRST EVIL* is want of water. There is no river in Arabia: and the small streams are often dried up by the heat.

The second evil is many locusts, which come in countless swarms, and devour every green thing.

The third evil is the burning winds. When a traveller feels it coming, he throws himself on the ground, covering his face with his cloak lest the hot sand should be blown up his nostrils. Sometimes the men and horses are choked by the sand.

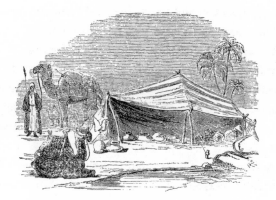

*YOU HAVE HEARD WHAT A DRY, DREARY, DESERT PLACE THE WILDERNESS WAS.*

These are the three evils: but there is a still greater—the religion of Mahomed: for this injures the soul; the other evils only hurt the body.

## TURKEY IN ASIA.

*Is THERE A* Turkey in Asia as well as a Turkey in Europe?

Yes, there is; and it is governed by the same Sultan, and filled by the same sort of persons. All Turks are Mahomedans.

When we look at a Mahomedan city we see, rising above the houses and trees, the domes and minarets of mosques.

Do you see the little narrow gallery outside the minaret? There is a man standing there. He is calling people to say their prayers. He calls so loud that all the people below can hear, and the sounds he utters are like sweet music. But would it not make you sad to hear them when you remembered what he was telling people to do? To pray to the God of Mahomet. Not to the God and Father of the Lord Jesus Christ, but to a FALSE god: to NO god.

Turkey in Asia used to be called Asia Minor (or Asia the less), and there it was that Paul the Apostle was born, and there he preached and turned many to Christ. But at last the Christians began to worship images, and the fierce Turks came and turned the churches into mosques. This was the punishment God sent the Christians for breaking His law.

How dreadful it would be if our churches should ever be turned into mosques! May God never send us this heavy punishment!

## KURDISTAN.

THE FIERCEST OF ALL THE PEOPLE in Asia are the Kurds.

They are the terror of all who live near them.

Their dwellings are in the mountains; there some live in villages, and some in black tents, and some in strong castles. At night they rush down from the mountains upon the people in the valleys, uttering a wild yell, and brandishing their swords. They enter the houses, and begin to pack up the things they find, and to place them on the backs of their mules and asses, while they drive away the cattle of the poor people; and if any one attempts to resist them, they kill him.

The reason why the Armenians live in holes in the ground is because they hope the Kurds may not find out where they are.

The Kurds have thin, dark faces, hooked noses, and black eyes, with a fierce and malicious look.

## MESOPOTAMIA.

THIS COUNTRY IS PART OF Turkey in Asia. It lies between two very famous rivers, the Tigris and the Euphrates, often spoken of in the Bible.

There is now a great city in Mesopotamia, called Bagdad. In Babylon no sound is heard but the howlings of wild *beasts*; in Bagdad *men* may be heard screaming and hallooing from morning to night. The drivers of the camels and mules shout as they press through the narrow, crooked streets, and even the ladies riding on white donkeys, and attended by black slaves, scream and holla.

# PERSIA.

In 1826, Russia scratched an imperialist itch by invading what's now Iran, giving itself a foothold in the Middle East. From 1834, the Russians and British found a suitably dependent Persian ruler in Mohammed Shah, who was compelled in 1846 to let Russia build ships at Resht and Astrabad. Mohammed's son, Nasr-ul-Din, succeeded him in September 1848, announcing energetic reforms and promising to lower taxes, although in practice he raised them even as he squandered public funds and allowed roads and bridges to go to seed. He survived an assassination attempt in August 1852. In July 1850, a young leader of the Bahá'i religion was executed in the public square of Tabriz; thousands of his followers were killed soon thereafter.

PERSIA IS NOW A MAHOMEDAN COUNTRY. The Turks you remember, are Mahomedans too. Perhaps you think these two nations, the Turks and the Persians, must agree well together, as they are of the same religion. Far from it. No nations hate one another more than Turks and Persians do; and the reason is, that though they both believe in Mahomet, they disagree about his son-in-law, Ali. The Persians are very fond of *him*, and keep a day of mourning in memory of his death: whereas the Turks do not care for Ali at all.

The Turks sit on sofas and lean against cushions; the Persians sit on carpets and lean against the wall. I know you would prefer the Turkish fashion.

Not only are their *customs* different, but their *characters*. The Turks are grave, and the Persians lively. The Turks are silent, the Persians talkative. The Turks are rude, the Persians polite. Now I am sure you like the Persians better than the Turks. But wait a little—the Turks are very proud; the Persians are very deceitful. An old Persian was heard to say, "We all tell lies whenever we can." The Persians are not even ashamed when their falsehoods are found out. When they sell they ask too much; when they make promises they break them. In short, it is impossible to trust a Persian.

**THE PERSIAN LADIES.**——They wrap themselves up in a large dark-blue wrapper, and in this dress they walk out where they please. No one who meets them can tell who they are.

And where do these women go? Chiefly to the bath, where they spend much of their time drinking coffee and smoking.

**PERSIAN INNS.**——They are very uncomfortable places. There are a great many small cells made of mud, built all round a large court. These cells are quite empty, and paved with stone. The only comfortable room is over the door-way of the court, and the first travellers who arrive are sure to settle in the room over the door-way.

**PILGRIMS AND BEGGARS.**——Very often you may see a large company of pilgrims, some on foot and some mounted on camels, horses, and asses. They are returning from Mecca, the birth-place of Mahomet. What good have they got by their pilgrimage? None at all. They think they are grown very holy, but they make such an uproar at the inns by quarrelling and fighting when they are travelling home, that no one can bear to be near them.

# C H I N A .

In the mid-nineteenth century, trade with the West wrenched China through some painful adjustments. A booming target audience of nearly four hundred million proved a tempting test market for Britain's socially and economically ruinous exports of illegal Indian opium. Chinese resistance to the trade and mutual hostilities led to the 1842 Treaty of Nanjing, ceding Hong Kong and five other ports to the British, and allowing the Brits some judicial autonomy in China—an arrangement echoed in later trade agreements with France and the United States. With the added pressures of droughts, floods, famine, and a rotting infrastructure, the Qing Dynasty came to face the Taiping Rebellion in 1851, a fourteen-year uprising that left some thirty million dead.

THERE IS NO COUNTRY in the world like China.

How different from Persia, where there are so few people; whereas China is crowded with inhabitants.

How different it is from England, where the people are instructed in the Bible: whereas China is full of idols.

China is a heathen country; yet it is not a savage country, for the people are quiet, and orderly, and industrious.

If you were to sit by a clock, and if all the Chinese were to pass before you one at a time, and if you were to count one at each tick of the clock, and if you were never to leave off counting day or night—how long do you think it would be before you had counted all the Chinese?

Twelve years. O what a vast number of people there must be in China! In all, there are about three hundred and sixty millions!

If all the people in the world were collected together, out of every three—one would be Chinese. How sad it is to think that this immense nation (except a few) knows not God, nor His glorious Son!

**FOOD.**—The poor can get nothing but rice to eat and water to drink; except now and then they mix a little pork or salt fish with their rice. Any sort of meat is thought good; even a hash of rats and snakes, or a mince of earth-worms. Cats' flesh and dogs' flesh are considered as nice as pork, and cost as much.

You will be surprised to hear that the Chinese are very fond of eating birds' nests. Do not suppose that they eat magpies' nests, which are made of clay and sticks, or even little nests of moss and clay: the nests they eat are made of a sort of gum. This gum comes out of the birds' mouths, and is shining and transparent, and the nests stick fast to the rock. These nests are something like our jelly, and must be very nourishing.

**APPEARANCE.**—A Chinaman does not take off his cap in company, and he has a good reason for it: his head is close shaven: only a long piece behind is allowed to grow, and this grows down to his heel, and is plaited. He wears a long dark-blue gown, with loose hanging sleeves. His shoes are clumsy, turned up at the toes in an ugly manner, and the soles are white. The Chinese have more trouble in whitening their shoes than we have in blacking ours.

The gentlemen are proud of having one long nail on the little finger, to show that they do not labour like the poor, for if they did, the nail would break. Men in China wear necklaces and use fans.

What foolish customs I have described.

**RELIGION.**—You have heard already that the Chinese worship the dead.

Who taught them this worship?

It was a man named Confucius, who lived a long while ago. This Confucius was a very wise man. From his childhood he was very fond of sitting alone, thinking, instead of playing with other children.

When he was fourteen he began to read some old books that had been written not long after the time of Noah. In these books he found very many wise sentences, such as Noah may have taught his own children. The Chinese had left off reading these wise books, and were growing more and more foolish. Confucius, when he was grown up, tried to persuade his countrymen to attend to the old books.

He was ill-treated by many of the rich and great, and he was so poor that rice was generally his only food. As soon as he was dead, people began to respect him highly, and even to worship him.

There is another religion in China besides that religion of Confucius, and a much worse religion. About the same time that Confucius lived, there was a man called La-on-tzee. He was a great deceiver, as you will see. He pretended that he could make people completely happy. There were three things, he said, he would do for them: first he would make them rich by turning stone into gold; next, he would prevent their being hurt by swords or by fire, through charms he could give them; and, last of all, he could save them from death by a drink he knew how to prepare.

What an awful liar this man must have been.

There is a *third* religion in China. It is the sect of Buddha. This Buddha was a man who once pretended to be turned into a god called Fo. You see he was even worse than La-on-tzee.

Buddha pretended that he could make people happy; and his way of doing so was very strange. He told them to think of nothing, and then they would be happy.

The Buddhists are full of tricks by which to get presents out of people.

Once a-year they cause a great feast to be made, and for whom? For the poor? No. For beasts? No. For children? No. For themselves? No. You will never guess. For ghosts! The priests declare that the souls of the dead are very hungry, and that it is right to give them a feast.

All the religions of China are bad, but of the three, the religion of Confucius is the least foolish.

The religion of Taou teaches men to act like madmen.

The religion of Buddha teaches them to act like idiots.

The religion of Confucius teaches them to act like wise men, but without souls.

**KNOWLEDGE AND INVENTIONS.**——We must allow that the Chinese are very clever. They found out how to print, and they found out how to make gunpowder, and they found out the use of the loadstone. What is that? A piece of steel rubbed against the loadstone will always point to the north. The Chinese found out these three things, printing, gunpowder, and the use of the loadstone, before we in Europe found them out. But they did not teach them to us; we found them out ourselves.

Schoolmasters are held in great honour in China, as, indeed, they *ought* to be *everywhere*. Yet schools in China are much like those in Turkey, more fit for parrots than children; only Chinese boys sit in chairs with desks before them, instead of sitting cross-legged on the ground as in Turkey. They learn first to paint the words, and next to repeat lessons by heart. This they do in a loud scream; always turning their backs to their master while they are saying their lessons to him.

**CHARACTER.**——A Chinaman's character cannot be known at first. You might suppose from his way of speaking, that a Chinaman was very humble; because he calls himself "the worthless fellow," or "the stupid one," and he calls his son "the son of a dog;" but if you were to tell him he had an evil heart, he would be very much offended: for he only gives himself these names that he may *seem* humble. The Chinese are proud of their country, and think there is none like it. They look upon foreigners as monkey and devils. Often a woman may be heard in the streets saying to her little child, "There is a foreign devil (or a Fan Quei")." The Chinese think the English very ugly, and call them the "red-haired nation."

The ladies who can live without working are very idle, and in the winter rise very late in the morning. Why should they rise early when they have nothing to do?

The Chinese are very selfish and unfeeling. Beggars may be seen in the middle of the town dying, and no one caring for them, but people gambling close by.

The Chinese used to be temperate, preferring tea to wine. There are tea-taverns in the towns. How much better than our beer-shops. But lately they have begun to smoke opium. This is the juice of the white poppy, made up into dark balls. The Chinese are not allowed to have it; but the English (sad to say) sell it to them secretly. There are many opium-taverns in China, where men may not be seen lying on cushions snuffing up the hot opium, and puffing it out of their mouths. Those who smoke opium have sunken cheeks and trembling

*THE RELIGION OF CONFUCIUS TEACHES MEN TO ACT LIKE WISE MEN, BUT WITHOUT SOULS.*

hands, and soon become old, foolish, and sick. Why, then, do they take opium? Many of them say they wish to leave it off, but cannot.

It is a common thing to stumble over the bodies of dead babies in the streets. In England it is counted murder to kill a babe, but it is thought no harm in China.

---

# HINDOSTAN.

The eighty million inhabitants of mid-nineteenth-century India were becoming more restive under objectionable land reforms, taxes, famine, and a general interference in local customs. Several years of unrest in the Punjab region culminated in the Battle of Gujarat; in February 1849, the Sikhs surrendered to Britain, and Britain annexed the territory a month later. (A more serious revolt would occur in 1857 and would take two years for the British to crush.) Economically, Britain was growing India quickly, with eleven thousand miles of telegraph lines and a fourteen-hundred-mile Grand Trunk road from Peshawar to Calcutta; rapid communication and irrigation were not yet considered up to snuff. One 1860s encyclopedia proclaimed that India's manufactured arts—fine textiles, rich embroideries, carved furniture, tapestries glittering with gems—were produced by "excessively dextrous" Hindus who nevertheless were "totally devoid of ingenuity."

WHAT A LARGE COUNTRY Hindostan is! Has it an emperor of its own as China has? No; large as it is, it belongs to the little country called England.

How did the English get it?

They conquered it little by little. When first they came there, they found a Mahomedan people, called the Moguls. These Moguls had conquered Hindostan; but by degrees the English conquered them, and became masters of all the land.

**APPEARANCE.**——The Hindoos are pleasing in their appearance, for their features are well-formed, their teeth are white, and their eyes have a soft expression. The women take much pains to dress their long black hair, which is soft as silk: they gather it up in a knot at the top of their heads, and crown it with flowers.

**FOOD.**——Water is the general drink, and there could not be a better. Yet there are intoxicating drinks, and some of the Hindoos have learned to love them, from seeing the English drink too much. What a sad thing that Christians should set a bad example to heathens!

**RELIGION.**——There is no nation that has so many gods as the Hindoos. What do you think of three hundred and thirty millions? There are not so many people in Hindostan as that. No one person can know the names of all these gods; and who would wish to know them? Some of them are snakes, and some are monkeys!

**THE CASTES.**——The priests are very proud of their high birth, and they call themselves Brahmins.

The labourers, who are told they come out of Brahma's foot, are much ashamed of their low birth. They are called sudras.

But the sudras are not the *most* despised people. Far from it. It is those who have no caste at all who are the most despised. They are called pariahs. These are people who have lost their caste. A Brahmin would lose his caste by eating with a sudra; a sudra would lose his by eating with a pariah, and by eating with *you*—yes, *you;* for the Hindoos think that no one is holy but themselves.

**BEGGARS.**——As you walk about Hindostan, you will sometimes meet a horrible object, with no other covering than a tiger's skin, or else an orange scarf; his body besmeared with ashes, his hair matted like the shaggy coat of a wild beast, and his nails like birds' claws. The man is a beggar, and a very bold one, because he is considered as one of the holiest of men. Who is he?

A sunyasse. Who is *he?*

A Brahmin, who wishing to be more holy than other Brahmins (holy as they are), has left all and become a beggar. It is wonderful to see the tortures which a sunyasse will endure. He will stand for years on one leg, till it is full of wounds, or if he prefer it, he will clench his fist till the nails grow through his hands.

There is another kind of beggars called fakirs; they are just as wicked and foolish as the sunyasses; but they are Mahomedans, and not Brahmins.

◇  ◇  ◇  ◇  ◇

## THE HINDOO WOMEN.

IT IS A MISERABLE THING to be a Hindoo lady. While she is a very little girl, she is allowed to play about, but when she comes to be ten or twelve years, she is shut up in the back rooms of the house till she is married; and when she is married she is still shut up. She may indeed walk in the garden at the back of the house, but nowhere else.

Hindoo ladies are not taught even those trifling accomplishments which Chinese ladies learn; they can neither paint, nor play music; much less can they read or write. They amuse themselves by putting on their ornaments, or by making curries and sweetmeats to please their husbands: but most of their time they spend in idleness, sauntering about and chattering nonsense.

\* \* \*

We have now described the two most numerous nations in the world, China and Hindostan. They contain together more than half the world. In some respects they are alike, and in some respects they are different.

| IN CHINA. | IN HINDOSTAN |
|---|---|
| There is one emperor. | There is no emperor, and the English govern the country. |
| They seldom wash themselves. | They bathe often. |
| They are grave and silent. | They are merry and talkative. |
| They are industrious. | They are idle. |

China and Hindostan are alike in these respects. They are both very *populous*, though China has twice as many inhabitants as Hindostan.

In both the women are shut up.

In both foreigners are hated.

In both the people are deceitful, unmerciful to the poor, and in the habit of destroying their own little girls as babies.

# CIRCASSIA.

The 1850s *Encyclopædia Britannica* describes Circassians as a "warlike, intrepid" people "characterized by hospitality and implacable vindictiveness." Already a Russian principality since the 1810s, Circassia was ceded to Russia by the Turks in the 1829 Treaty of Adrianople, and the "warlike, intrepid" locals would fight the motherland for decades to come.

*CIRCASSIA, THOUGH BEAUTIFUL,*
*IS AN UNHAPPY COUNTRY.*

THIS IS NOT A VAST COUNTRY like China, or Hindostan. It may be called a nook, it is so small compared with some great kingdoms: but it is famous on account of the beauty of its people. They are fair, like Europeans, with handsome features and fine figures. But their beauty has done them harm, and not good; for the cruel Turks purchase many of the Circassian women, because they are beautiful, and shut them up in their houses.

**MANNERS OF THE PEOPLE.**——There is no country in the world where the people are as kind to strangers as in Circassia. Every family, however poor, has a guest-house. The wind may whistle through the chinks, and the rain come through the roof, but the stranger is well warmed, and comfortably lodged; and above all, he has the host to wait upon him with more attention than a servant.

**THE CIRCASSIAN MEN.**——War is their chief occupation. Working in the fields is left to the women, and the little boys, and the slaves. There is, alas! great occasion for the men to fight, as the land has long been infested with many dangerous enemies.

The Russians are endeavouring to conquer the Circassians: but the Circassians declare they will die sooner than yield. Every man carries a gun, a pistol, a dagger, and a sword; and the nobles are distinguished by a bow and a quiver of arrows.

The boys are taught from their infancy to be hardy and manly. Instead of remaining at home, they are given, at three years old, into the care of a stranger. The boy follows his foster-father over the mountains, urging his horse to climb tremendous heights, and to rush down dark ravines; and appeasing his hunger with a mouthful of honey from the bag fastened to his girdle. Such is the life he leads till he is a tall and strong youth; and then he returns home to his parents.

Men brought up in this manner must be wild, bold, restless, and ignorant. Such are the Circassians.

**THE GOVERNMENT.**——The Circassians admire sweet winning speeches. They say there are three things which mark a great man; a sharp sword, a sweet tongue, and forty tables. What do they mean by these? By a sharp sword they mean bravery;—by a sweet tongue they mean soft speeches;—and by forty tables they mean giving plentiful suppers to neighbours and to strangers. Are the Circassians right in this way of thinking? No—for their bravery is good, and speaking well is good, and giving away is good—these are not the greatest virtues; and people may be brave, and speak well, and give away much, and yet be wicked; for they may be without the love of God in their hearts.

**RELIGION.**——Circassia, though beautiful, is an unhappy country. The Russians keep the people in continual fear; this is a great evil. But there is another nation who have done the Circassians still greater harm. I mean the Turks. And what have they done to them? They have persuaded them to turn Mahomedans. The greatest harm that can be done to any one, is to give him a false religion.

# GEORGIA.

In 1854, Britain and France began to interfere with the human trafficking of young Circassian men and women by Georgian nobles, who sold athletic males as soldiers and beautiful females as concubines. "From this horrid traffic," noted an *Encyclopædia Britannica* entry of the late 1850s, "the Georgian nobles long derived their chief revenue." Georgia's 1855 population was estimated at six hundred thousand, with the seat of commerce and government in Tiflis.

GEORGIA IS FAR MORE FRUITFUL than Circassia, the people too, are less fair, and less industrious.

While Circassian ladies are busy weaving and milking, the Georgian ladies loll upon their couches, and do nothing. Which do you think are the happier? These Georgian ladies, too, though very handsome, are much disfigured by painted faces and stained eye-brows. Their countenances, too, are lifeless, and silly, as might be expected, since they waste their time in idleness.

There is no country where so much wine is drunk as in Georgia, even a labourer is allowed five bottles a day.

---

# TARTARY.

The agricultural nineteenth-century Tartars, living in what would become Mongolia, Siberia, and other regions of Central Asia, strenuously resisted Russian conquest, although some societies lived among Russians. The *Encyclopædia Britannica* reported that the Tcholyms spoke a Turkish dialect incorporating Mongol and Yakut words, and that two other societies, the Altai and the Kalmucks, had nothing in common apart from dress and lifestyle.

NOTHING CAN BE SO DREARY as the steppes appear in winter time. The high wind sweeping along the plain, drives the snow into high heaps, and often hurls the poor animals into a cold grave. Sledges cannot be used, because they cannot slide on the ground. But if the *white* ground looks dreary in winter, the *black* ground looks hideous in summer; for the hot sun turns the grass black, and fills the air with black dust, and there are no shady groves, no cool hills, no refreshing brooks. **WILD ANIMALS.**—There are some very odious animals on the steppe. Snakes and toads. Yes, showers of toads sometimes fall. But neither snakes nor toads are as great a plague as locusts. These little animals, not bigger than a child's thumb, are more to be dreaded than a troop of wolves. And why? In the first warm days of spring the young animals come forth, and immediately they begin crawling on the ground in one immense flock, eating up all the grass as they pass along; in a month they can fly, and then they darken the air like a thick cloud; wherever any green appears, they drop down and settle on the spot.

**PEOPLE AND CUSTOMS.**—Every six weeks the Tartars move to a new place. It is great labour to the Tartar women to pack up the tents and to place them on the backs of the camels, and then to unpack and to pitch the tents. It is a great disgrace to the men to suffer the women to work as hard as they do; but the men are very idle, and like to sit by their tents smoking and drinking, while their wives are toiling and striving with all their might.

**APPEARANCE.**—The Tartars are not handsome like the Turks and Circassians. They are short and thick; their faces are broad and bony, their eyes very small, and only half open; their noses flat, their lips thick, their chins pointed, their ears large and flapping, and their skin dark and yellow.

❖  ❖  ❖  ❖  ❖

## BOKHARA (IN TARTARY).

*THIS IS A KINGDOM* in the midst of Tartary. It lies at the south of the Caspian Sea. It is not like the rest of Tartary, for it is a sweet green spot. Travellers have said that it is the most beautiful spot in the world, but that is not true. The reason that travellers have said so, is that, after passing through a great desert, they have been charmed at seeing again running streams and shady groves.

But though Bokhara is a beautiful place, it is a wicked place.

The king is one of the greatest tyrants in the world. He is called the Amir.

He lives in constant fear of his life.

The Amir's dinner, when it is ready, is not placed on the royal table, but locked up in a box, and taken to the Vizier to be tasted, before it is served up in the palace.

But it is not the Amir only who is afraid of poison. No one will accept fruit from another, unless that other tastes it first. It must be very terrible to live in the midst of such murderers as the people of Bokhara seem to be.

**RELIGION.**——Bokhara is reckoned by Mahomedans a very religious city; for in every street there is a mosque; every evening people may be seen crowding to prayers; and if boys are caught asleep during service, they are tied together, and driven round the market by an officer, who beats them all the way with a thick thong.

There is a school, too, in almost every street of Bokhara, and there the poor boys sit, from sunrise till an hour before sunset, bawling out their foolish lessons from the Koran; and during all that time they are never allowed to go home, except once for some bread. They have no time for play, except in the evening, and no holiday except on Friday.

✧ ✧ ✧ ✧ ✧

## THE TOORKMAN TARTARS.

YOU HAVE HEARD A GREAT DEAL of the Tartars, and you have been told that they are a quiet and peaceful nation. But not *all;* there is a tribe of Tartars called the Toorkmans, of a very different character.

Robbery is their whole business. For this purpose they learn to ride and to fight. They understand well how to manage a horse, so as to make him strong and swift.

It is not surprising that the Toorkmans do not eat these thin horses. They prefer mutton. When they invite a stranger to dinner, they boil a whole sheep in a large boiling-pot; then tear up the flesh,—mix it with crumbled bread, and serve it up in wooden bowls. Two persons eat from one bowl, dipping their hands into it, and licking up their food like dogs.

The tents are adorned with beautiful carpets; not only the floors, but the sides, and it is the chief employment of the women to weave them. As for the men, they spend most of their time in sauntering about among the tents; for the fierce dogs guard the flocks. But when their hands are idle, their thoughts are still busy in planning new robberies and murders.

---

# *AFFGHANISTAN.*

In the early 1840s, independence-minded Afghanistan resisted the expansionist aims of Russia and Britain, fending off sixteen thousand soldiers (and killing nearly every one of them) during the first Anglo-Afghan war, between 1839 and 1842. The British-installed ruler, Shah Shuja, was assassinated in 1842, and deposed emir Dost Mahommed recovered Kabul. The Afghans sided with the Sikhs during Punjabi conflicts with the British in 1846, but deserted them three years later in the Battle of Gujarat, when the Anglo-Indian army defeated the Sikhs and retook the Khyber Pass. With the 1855 signing of the Treaty of Peshawar, the British and the Afghans buried the hatchet—at least for the time being.

*THIS LAND IS NOT A DESERT.* Yet there are but few trees, and because there is so little shade, the rivulets are soon dried up. Yet it might be a fruitful land, if the inhabitants would plant and sow. But

they prefer wandering about in tents, and living upon plunder, to settling in one place and living by their labour. The Tartar has good
reason for roaming over his plains, because the land is bad; but the
Affghan has no reason, but the *love* of roaming.

The men are terrible-looking creatures, tall, large, dark, and grim,
with shaggy hair and long black beards. They wear great turbans of
blue check, and handsome jackets, and cloaks of sheep-skin; they
carry in their girdles knives as large as a butcher's, and on their
shoulders a shield and a gun.

Cabool, the capital, is a fine city, and the king dwells in a fine
citadel.

The noise in the city is so great that it is difficult to make a friend

*THE MEN ARE TERRIBLE-LOOKING CREATURES.*

hear what you say: it is not the noise of rumbling wheels, as in London, for there are no wheeled carriages, but the noise of chattering tongues.

The Affghan, though living on fruits, is far from being a harmless and amiable character; on the contrary, he is cruel, covetous, and treacherous. Much British blood has been shed in the valleys of Affghanistan.

We cannot blame the Affghans for defending their own country. It was natural for them to ask, "What right has Britain to interfere with us?"

A British Army was once sent to Affghanistan to force the people to have a king they did not like, instead of one they did like.

---

# BURMAH.

Britain's violent 1826 colonization of Burma (today called Myanmar, sometimes), which was ruled by non-hereditary absolute despots, sparked years of sullen resentment, leading to violence against British ships and sailors in the 1840s, and finally, all-out war in January 1852. The British stormed Rangoon (now Yangon) in June of that year and annexed the southern city of Pegu in December; in February 1853, Prince Mendoon overthrew and imprisoned King Pagán-Men. Rangoon suffered a devastating fire that year as well. Trade by overland routes was restored between China and British Burma in 1855.

OF ALL THE KINGS IN ASIA, the king of Burmah is the greatest, next to the emperor of China. He is called "Lord of life and death," and the "Owner of the sword," for instead of holding a *sceptre* in his hand, he holds a golden sheathed *sword*. A sword indeed suits him well, for he is very cruel to his subjects. Nowhere are such severe punishments inflicted. For drinking brandy the punishment is, pouring molten lead down the throat; and for running away from the army, the punishment is, cutting off both legs, and leaving the poor creature to bleed to death.

Every one is much afraid of offending this cruel king.

Though the Burmese are so unfeeling to each other, they think it wrong to kill animals, and never eat any meat, except the flesh of animals that have died of themselves. Even the fishermen think they shall be punished hereafter for catching fish; but they say, "We must do it, or we shall be starved." You may be sure that such a people must have some false and foolish religion; and so they have, as you will see.

**RELIGION.**—It is the religion of Buddha. The Burmese do not think he is alive now; they say he is resting as a reward for his goodness. Why, then, do they pray to him, if he cannot hear them? They pray because they think it is very good to pray, and that they shall be rewarded for it some day. What reward do they expect? It is this—to *rest* as Buddha does—to sleep for ever and ever. This is the reward they look for.

**CHARACTER.**—The Burmese are a blunt and rough people. They are not like the Chinese, and the Hindoos, ready to pay compliments to strangers. When a Burmese has finished a visit, he says, "I am going," and his friend replies, "Go." This is very blunt behaviour. But all blunt people are not sincere. The Burmese are very deceitful, and tell lies on every occasion; indeed, they are not ashamed of their falsehoods. They are also very proud, because they fancy they were so good before they were born into this world.

The Burmese resemble the Chinese in their respect to their parents. They are temperate also, not drinking wine,—having only two meals in the day, and then not eating too much. They are, however, very violent in their tempers; it is true they are not very easily provoked, but when they are angry they use very abusive language. Thus, you see, they are by no means an amiable people.

**APPEARANCE.**—In their persons they are far less pleasing than the Hindoos; for instead of *slender* faces and figures, they have broad faces and thick figures. But they have not such dark complexions as the Hindoos.

They disfigure themselves in various ways. To make their skins yellow, they sprinkle over them a yellow powder. They also make their teeth black, because they say they do not wish to have white teeth, like dogs and monkeys.

# S I A M .

Thailand expanded its trade with the West in the 1850s, sowing the seeds of a vast commercial expansion, after King Mongkut ascended to the throne in 1851. Bangkok was trying to regain its status as Asia's third-most commercial city (behind Calcutta and Guangzhou, then called Canton), eroded by years of bad legislation and destructive monopolies. But in contrast with its Burmese neighbors, the Siamese signed an 1855 treaty of friendship and commerce with the British, letting the Westerners trade at Siamese ports, buy local property, and practice Christianity. Only twelve ships arrived annually before the treaty; by 1863, eighty-two ships docked here each year. And agriculture advanced in the decade after 1855, when farmers were using buffalo to turn the soil.

CROSS A RIVER, and you pass from Burmah to Siam. These two countries, like most countries close together, have quarreled a great deal, and now Britain has got in between them, and has parted them: as a nurse might come and part two quarrelsome children.

But though these two countries have been such enemies, they are as like each other as two sisters. Siam is the little sister.

THE SIAMESE RESEMBLE THE BURMESE IN APPEARANCE,
BUT THEY ARE MUCH WORSE-LOOKING.

The Siamese resemble the Burmese in appearance, but they are much worse-looking. Their faces are very broad and flat; and so large are the jaws under the ears, that they appear as if they were swollen. Their manner of dressing their hair does not improve their looks; for they cut their hair quite close, except just on the top of their heads, where they make it stand up like bristles; nor do they wear any covering on their heads, except when it is very hot, and then they put on a hat made of leaves, in the shape of a milk-pan.

In disposition the Siamese are deceitful and cowardly. It has been said of them, that as *friends* they are not to be *trusted*, and as *enemies* not to be *feared:* they cannot be trusted, because they are deceitful: they need not be feared, because they are cowardly.

The Siamese are like the Burmese in cruelty. When an enemy falls into their hands, no mercy is shown.

A king of a small country, called Laos, was taken captive by the Siamese. This king, with his family, was shut up in a large iron cage, and exhibited as a sight. There he was, surrounded by his sons and grandsons, and all of them heavily laden with chains on their necks and legs. Two of them were little boys, and they played and laughed in their cage!—so thoughtless are children! But the elder sons looked very miserable; they hung down their heads, and fixed their eyes on the ground; and well they might; for within their sight were various horrible instruments of torture;—spears with which to pierce them;—an iron boiler in which to heat oil to scald them;—a gallows on which to hang their bodies, and—a pestle and mortar in which to pound the children to powder. You see how Satan fills the heart of the heathen with his own cruel devices.

What became of the unhappy family is not known.

But though so barbarous to their *enemies*, the Siamese in some respects are better than most heathen nations, for they treat their *relations* more kindly. They do not kill their infants, nor shut up their wives, nor cast out their parents. Yet they show their cruelty in this:—they often sell one another for slaves.

❖  ❖  ❖  ❖  ❖

## BANKOK.

THIS CITY IS BUILT ON AN ISLAND in a broad river, and part of it on the banks of the river. It ought therefore to be a pleasant city, but it is *not,* owing to its extreme untidiness. The streets are full of mud, and overgrown with bushes, amongst which all the refuse is thrown; there are also many ditches with planks thrown across. There is only one pleasant part of the town, and that is where the Wats are built. The Wats are the idol-houses. Near them are shady walks in fragrant flowers, and elegant dwellings for the priests. The people think they get great merit by making wats, and therefore they take so much trouble: for the Siamese are very idle. So idle are they, that there would be very little trade in Bankok if it were not for the Chinese, who come over here in crowds, and make sugar, and buy and sell, and get money to take back to China.

---

# MALACCA.

By the 1840s, the feverish Dutch trade in what would become Indonesia and Malaysia had inflamed the envy of British merchants, who muscled in on the territory's rice, pepper, timber, tin, and diamonds. In 1841, the Sultan of Brunei bestowed a new title—the Rajah of Sarawak—upon English adventurer Sir James Brooke, who had helped quell a local rebellion, and guaranteed the safety of British trade in Borneo. In September 1851, the British administration of Bengal annexed the ports of Singapore and Malacca (later Kuala Lumpur), along with Prince of Wales Island (later Penang).

THE WEATHER IN MALACCA is much pleasanter than in most parts of India, because the sea-breezes make the air fresh.

Yet it is a dangerous country to live in, for the people are very treacherous. There are many pirates among them. The governors of the land do not punish the pirates; far from punishing them they share in the gains. That is a wicked land indeed, where the governors encourage the people in their sins.

There are some valuable plants in Malacca. Who collects the pepper and the sago? There are mines of tin. Who digs up the tin? The idle Malays will not take so much trouble, so the industrious Chinese labour instead. The Chinese come over by thousands to get rich in Malacca. But though the Chinese set an example of *industry*, they do not set an example of *goodness;* for they gamble, and so lose their *money:* they smoke opium, and so lose their *health;* and they commit many kinds of wickedness, by which they lose their *souls*.

As for the Malays, they are so very idle, that when trees fall over the river and block up the way, they will not be at the trouble of cutting a way through for their boats,—but will sooner creep *under* or climb *over* the fallen trees.

The capital of Malacca is Malacca, and this city belongs to the English; but it is of little use to them, because the harbour is not good.

# $S\ I\ B\ E\ R\ I\ A$ .

In the nineteenth century, many of the region's 5.4 million people were colonists in search of religious freedom, although some seventy thousand misbehaving peasants were transported to the steppe between 1832 and 1842. Siberia's only significant trades were spirits and leather, though iron mining was on the rise. Other, more minor trades included soap-boiling, tallow-melting, and Ural River fishing of beluga, noted at the time for its "delicate" caviar.

*THIS IS A NAME* which makes people *shiver*, because it reminds them of the cold. It is a name which makes the Russians *tremble*, because it reminds them of banishment, for the emperor often sends those who offend him to live in Siberia.

**INHABITANTS.**——The Russians are the masters of Siberia, and they have built several large towns there. But these towns are very far apart, and there are many wild tribes wandering about the country.

One of these tribes is the Ostyaks.

The Ostyak wears a great coat made of the skin of a white deer; this gives him the appearance of a great white bear.

What a wild creature the Ostyak must look, when he is hunting his prey, wrapped in his shaggy white coat,——his long dark hair floating in the wind——his enormous bow in his hand, and his enormous shoes on his feet!

What is the character of this wild man? Ask what is his religion, and that will show you how foolish and fierce a creature he must be. The Ostyak says, that he believes in ONE God who cannot be seen, but he does not worship him *alone;* he worships other gods. And such gods? Dead men!

But what do you think of men worshipping DEAD BEASTS? Yet this is what the Ostyaks do. When they have killed a wolf or a bear, they stuff its skin with hay, and gather round to mock it, to kick it, to spit upon it, and then——they stick it up on its hind legs in a corner of the hut, and worship it! Alas! how has Satan blinded their mind!

The Russians do much harm to their subjects, by tempting them to buy brandy. There is nothing which the Ostyaks are so eager to obtain as this dangerous drink.

❖ ❖ ❖ ❖ ❖

## THE SAMOYEDES.

*THEY ARE A MUCH WILDER PEOPLE* than the Ostyaks. The women dress in a stranger, fantastic manner: not contented with a rein-deer dress, as the Ostyaks are, they join furs and skins of various sorts together; and instead of veiling their faces, they wear a gay fur hat, with lappets; and at the back of their necks a glutton's tail hangs down, as well as long tails of their own hair, with brass rings jingling together at the end.

But if their taste in *dress* is laughable, their taste in *food* is horrible, as you will see. A traveller went with a Samoyede family for a little while.

One day the traveller saw a Samoyede feast. A rein-deer was brought, and killed before the tent door; and its bleeding body was taken into the tent, and devoured, all raw as it was, with the heartiest appetite. It was dreadful to see the Samoyedes gnawing the flesh off the bones; their faces all stained with blood, and even the child had his share of the raw meat. Truly they looked more like wolves than men.

## *CEYLON.*

The resources of this Indian Ocean island, later Sri Lanka, were first noticed in 1505 by the Portuguese, whose missionary zeal was roundly despised by the indigenous Cingalese and Tamils. The Dutch arrived in 1603 and were soon hated equally for instituting Cingalese forced labor in the interior highlands around Kandy and the monopolization of the cinnamon trade. Britain colonized Ceylon in 1802, tapping its rich veins of precious stones, cinnamon, rice, tea, and coffee; by the mid-nineteenth century, new coffee plantations were rapidly replacing the rainforest. The British suppressed an 1848 tax rebellion in Kandy. The island's revenue was £569,047 in 1857, when twenty-five thousand Europeans lived among the nearly 1.7 million locals.

*THIS IS ONE OF THE MOST BEAUTIFUL ISLANDS* in the world. Part of it indeed is flat—that part near Hindostan; but in the midst—there are mountains; and streams running down their sides, and swelling into lovely rivers, winding along the fruitful valleys. Such scenes might remind you of Switzerland, the most beautiful country in Europe.

*NO WONDER THAT THE PROUD KING HAD ENEMIES, FOR HE WAS A MONSTER OF CRUELTY.*

**PEOPLE.**——And who are the people who live in this beautiful island?

In the flat part of the island, towards the north, the people resemble the Hindoos, and speak and think like them; and they are called Tamuls.

But among the mountains of the south a different kind of people live, called the Cingalese. They do not speak the Tamul language, nor do they follow the Hindoo religion. They follow the Buddhist religion.

There is another worship in Ceylon, and it is more followed than the worship of Buddha, yet it is the most horrible that you can imagine. It is the worship of the DEVIL!!

There are many *devil priests*. When any one is sick, it is supposed that the devil has caused the sickness, and a devil-priest is sent for. And what can the priest do? He dances,—he sings,—with his face painted,—small bells upon his legs,—and a flaming torch in each hand; while another man beats a loud drum. All this he does to please the devil, and to coax him to come out of the sick person. This is what he *pretends;*—but in *reality,* he seeks to get money by his tricks.

❖  ❖  ❖  ❖  ❖

## KANDY.

*THIS TOWN IS BUILT* among the high mountains. It was built there for the same reason that the eagle builds her nest on the top of a tall rock,—to get out of the reach of enemies. But the proud king, who once dwelt there, has been conquered, and now England's Queen rules over Ceylon. No wonder that the proud king had enemies, for he was a monster of cruelty. His palace is still to be seen. See that high tower, and that open gallery at the top! There the *last king* used to stand to enjoy the sight of his subjects' agonies. Those who had offended him were killed in the court below,—killed not in a common manner, but in all kinds of barbarous ways,—such as by being cut in pieces, or by swallowing melted lead.

# BORNEO.

Though the Dutch had hoped to colonize Borneo, the sultan agreed in 1847 to cede no more territory without the consent of Britain, which promptly annexed the island. Sir James Brooke was named governor of the colony in October 1848. The Dutch crushed a revolt in nearby Java in 1849.

THIS IS THE LARGEST ISLAND in the world, except one. Borneo is a heathen island. Yet Borneo is not an island of *idols*, as Ceylon is. *All* heathens do not worship idols.

Many people have come from Malacca, and settled in Borneo; so the island is full of Malays. These people have a cunning and cruel look, and no wonder;—for many of them are PIRATES! It is a common custom in Borneo to go out in a large boat,—to watch for smaller boats,—and to bring them home as slaves. There are no seas in the world so dangerous to sail in as the seas near Borneo, not only on account of the rocks, but on account of the great number of pirates.

❖  ❖  ❖  ❖  ❖

## THE DYAKS.

THESE ARE A SAVAGE PEOPLE who inhabit Borneo. They lived there before the Malays came, and they have been obliged to submit to them. They are savages indeed. They are darker than the Malays; yet they are not black; their skin is only the colour of copper. They wear very little clothing, but they adorn their ears, and arms, and legs, with numbers of brass rings. Their looks are wild and fierce, but not cunning, like the looks of the Malays.

Their wickedness is very great. It is their chief delight to get the heads of their enemies. There are a great many different tribes of Dyaks, and each tribe tries to cut off the heads of other tribes. The Dyaks who live by the sea are the most cruel; they go out in the boats to rob, and to bring home, not *slaves*, but HEADS!

The man who has *most* heads is considered the *greatest* man. A man who has NO HEADS is despised! If he wishes to be respected, he must get a head as soon as he can.

People who are so bent on killing, as these Dyaks are, must have many enemies. The Dyaks are always in fear of being attacked by their enemies.

---

# *J A P A N .*

In 1854, U.S. Commodore Matthew C. Perry's signature on the Treaty of Kanagawa established a limited trading partnership with this society, which had previously kept its distance from the West. The largely agricultural Japan stepped up its tea and silk exports to the Americans, British, French, Russians—and the Dutch, who agreed to halt monopolistic trade conditions after the treaty. Japan's estimated thirty-three million inhabitants were ruled by a spiritual emperor, the reigning Mikado, and a secular emperor, the governing Tycoon, who oversaw a feudalistic economic system kept in check by extensive surveillance and espionage. Hari-Kari, the belly cut, was a "most remarkable custom," according to an 1863 encyclopedia, which also noted that husbands could legally execute adulterous wives.

*THIS IS THE NAME* of a great empire. There are three principal islands. The three islands *together* are larger than our island. There is a fourth island near the Japan islands, called Jesso, and it is filled with Japanese people.

I shall not be able to tell you much about Japan; as strangers may not go there, nor natives come from it. English ships very seldom go to Japan, because they are so closely watched.

What sort of people are the Japanese?

They are a very polite people,—much politer than the Chinese,—but very proud. They are a learned nation, for they can read and write, and they understand geography, arithmetic, and astronomy.

The climate is pleasant, for the winter is short, and the sun is not as hot as in China; so that the ladies, and gentlemen, are almost as fair as Europeans, though the labourers are very dark.

But Japan is exposed to many dangers, from wind, from water, and from fire—three terrible enemies! The waves dash with violence upon the rocky shores; the wind often blows in fearful hurricanes; while earthquakes and hot streams from the burning mountains, fill the people with terror.

But more terrible than any of these—is wickedness; and very wicked customs are observed in Japan. It is very wicked for a man to kill himself, yet in Japan it is the custom for all courtiers who have offended the emperor, to cut open their own bodies with a sword. The little boys of five years old, begin to learn the dreadful art. They do not really cut themselves, but they are shown *how* to do it, that when they are men, they may be able to kill themselves in an elegant manner. How dreadful!

# AUSTRALIA.

Although Britain's former prime minister Lord John Russell stopped sending convicts here in February 1853, a gold rush echoing that of the American West nearly tripled the young country's population in the 1850s. A California prospector named Edward Hargreaves discovered gold in April 1851 at Summerhill Creek, near Bathurst, some two hundred miles west of Sydney; three months later, an aboriginal miner located another rich vein at Anderson's Creek, near Melbourne. By 1852, prospectors abandoning once-productive copper mines—and arriving in Melbourne from Europe, America, New Zealand, China, and Tasmania, at a rate of two thousand per week—had struck 105 tons, valued at £8.8 million. The not-quite-so-bullish wool market produced forty-five million pounds in 1852.

THIS IS THE LARGEST ISLAND in the world. It is as large as Europe (which is not an *island*, but a *continent*). But how different is Australia from Europe! Instead of containing, as Europe does, a number of grand kingdoms, it has not one single king. Instead of being filled with people, the greater part of Australia is a desert, or a forest, where a few half naked savages are wandering.

Australia is not so fine a land as Europe, because it has not so many fine rivers; and it is fine *rivers* that make a fine *land*. Most of the rivers in Australia do not deserve the name of rivers; they are more like a number of watering holes, and are often dried up in the summer, but there is one very fine, broad, long, deep river, called the Murray. It flows for twelve hundred miles. Were there several such rivers as the Murray, then Australia would be a fine land indeed.

**THE NATIVES.**——The savages of Australia have neither god, nor king. Some heathen countries are full of idols, but there are no idols in the wilds of Australia. No,—like the beasts which perish, these savages live from day to day without prayer or praise, delighting only in eating and drinking, hunting and dancing.

The women are the most ill-treated creatures in the world. The men beat them on their heads whenever they please, and cover them with bruises.

The miserable "gins" (for that is the name for a *wife* or *woman*) are not *beaten* only; they are *half starved;* for their husbands will give them no food, and *they*—poor things—cannot fish, or hunt, or shoot; they have nothing but the roots they dig up, and the grubs, and lizards, and snakes they find on the ground.

I have already told you that the natives have no GOD; yet they have a DEVIL, whom they call Yakoo, or debbil-debbil. Of him they are always afraid, for they fancy he goes about devouring children.

These savages show themselves to be children of debbil-debbil by their actions. They kill many of their babes, that they may not have the trouble of nursing them. Old people also they kill, and laugh at the idea of making them "tumble down." One of the most horrible things they do, is making the skulls of their friends into drinking-cups, and they think that, by doing so, they show their AFFECTION!! They allow the nearest relation to have the skull of the dead person. They will even EAT a little piece of the dead body, just as a mark of love. But, generally speaking, it is only their *enemies* they eat, and they *do* eat them whenever they can kill them.

But though these savages are so wicked, and so wild, they have their amusements. Dancing is the chief amusement. At every full moon, there is a grand dance, called the Corrobory. It is the men who dance, while the women sit by and beat time. Nothing can be more horrible to see than a Corrobory. It is held in the night by the light of blazing fires.

The men are made to look more frightful than usual, by great patches and stripes of red and white clay all over their bodies; and they play all manner of strange antics, and utter all kinds of strange yells; so that you might think it was a dance in HELL, rather than on earth.

It may surprise you to hear, these wild creatures have a turn both for music and drawing. Figures have been found carved upon the rocks, which show their turn for drawing. These figures represent beasts, fishes, and men, and are much better done than could have been supposed. There are few savages who can sing as well as these natives, but the *words* of their songs are very foolish. These are the words of one song:—

> "Eat great deal; eat, eat, eat:
> Eat again; plenty to eat:
> Eat more yet; eat, eat, eat."

If a pig could sing, surely this song would just suit its fancy.

And what is the appearance of these people?

They are ugly, with flat noses and wide mouths, but their teeth are white, and their hair is long, glossy, and curly. They adorn their tresses with teeth, and feathers, and dogs' tails; and they rub over their whole body—fish-oil and fat. You may imagine, therefore, how unpleasant it must be to come near them.

❖ ❖ ❖ ❖ ❖

## THE COLONISTS OR SETTLERS.

THERE ARE TWO SORTS of white people who have come to Australia. They are called "Convicts," and "Colonists."

Convicts are some of the worst of the white people;—thieves, who instead of being kept in prison, were sent to Australia to work hard for many years.

Colonists are people who come of their own accord to earn their living as best they can.

But there are *men*, called "bush-rangers," as fierce as wild beasts. These are convicts who have escaped from punishment. They often come to the settlers' houses, and murder the inhabitants.

The natives are not nearly so dangerous as these wicked *white* men; indeed the natives are generally very harmless, unless provoked by ill-treatment. They are willing to make themselves useful, by reaping corn, and washing sheep: and a little reward satisfies them, such as a blanket, or an old coat. The black women can help in the wash-house, and in the farm-yard; but they are too much besmeared with grease to be fit for the kitchen. It is wise never to give a good dinner to a black till his work is done, because he always eats so much that he can work no more that day.

❖  ❖  ❖  ❖  ❖

## BOTANY BAY.

*THIS IS A FAMOUS PLACE*, for here the English first settled, and here it was—thieves were sent from England as punishment. How did the place get the beautiful name of Botany? which means, "the knowledge of flowers." Because there were so many beautiful flowers seen there, when Captain Cook first beheld it. Yet the name, Botany Bay, does not seem beautiful to us; for it reminds us not of roses, but of rogues; not of violets, but of violent men; not of lilies, but of villains.

❖  ❖  ❖  ❖  ❖

## SYDNEY.

*THIS TOWN IS CLOSE* to Botany Bay.

It is the largest town in Australia. It is a very wicked city; because so many convicts have been sent there. Numbers of the people are the children of convicts, and have been brought up very ill by their parents. Of course there are many robberies in such a city, far more than there are in London. Who would like to live there! yet it is a fine city, and by the sea-side, with a harbour, where hundreds of ships might ride,—safe from the storm.

❖ ❖ ❖ ❖ ❖

## ADELAIDE.

*IT IS MUCH BETTER* to live here than in Sydney, because convicts have never been sent here. Numbers of honest poor people are leaving England and Ireland, every year, to go to Adelaide.

But there is one great evil both in Sydney and in Adelaide, which is the dust blown from the desert, and which almost chokes the inhabitants.

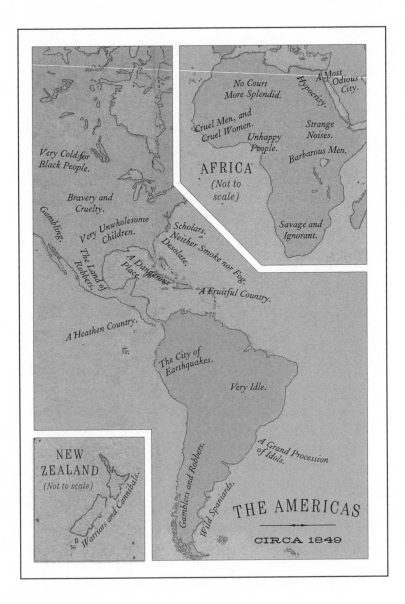

Very Cold for
Black People.

No Court
More Splendid.

Hypocrisy.

A Most
Odious
City.

Cruel Men, and
Cruel Women.

Strange
Noises.

Unhappy
People.

Barbarous Men.

AFRICA
(Not to
scale)

Bravery and
Cruelty.

Gambling.

Very Unwholesome
Children.

The Land of
Robbers.

Scholars.
Neither Smoke nor Fog.

Desolate.

A Dangerous
Place.

A Fruitful Country.

Savage and
Ignorant.

A Heathen Country.

The City of
Earthquakes.

Very Idle.

NEW
ZEALAND
(Not to
scale)

Warriors and Cannibals.

Gamblers and Robbers.

Wild Spaniards.

A Grand Procession
of Idols.

THE AMERICAS

CIRCA 1849

## PART III

# THE
# WICKEDEST
# CITY
# IN THE
# WORLD;

SELECTIONS FROM

*Far Off, Part II:*
*Africa and America Described,*

with Anecdotes and
Numerous Illustrations,

1854.

# AFRICA.

———————•••———————

*THIS IS THE MOST UNHAPPY* of the four quarters of the globe. It is the land whence more slaves come than from any other; it may be called the land of bondage.

It is the hottest of all the quarters of the globe. In many places it seldom rains, and the streams are dried up.

It is less well-known than any other continent. There are mountains and lakes of immense size, which white men have never seen.

The blackest people in the world are born in Africa.

There are more ignorant people there than anywhere else;—people who cannot read or write; and also people who know nothing of Jesus, the Son of God.

———————•••———————

# *E G Y P T .*

Mohammed Ali, once an Albanian officer in the Turkish army, enjoyed absolute rule for several decades as Egypt's viceroy, under the auspices of the Ottomans. He rapidly built European-modeled schools, railways, canals, factories, courts, and armed forces, although in 1840 the British forcefully reduced Egypt's military forces and autonomy. Mohammed Ali died in August 1849, when his grandson Abbas Pasha began a five-year rule. Abbas's successor, Said Pasha, oversaw a French company's groundbreaking of the Suez Canal in 1859 (a "seemingly impracticable enterprise," sniffed an 1862 encyclopedia). Alexandria was a boomtown: 2.5 million inhabitants in 1844 grew to more than five million by 1859.

THIS COUNTRY IS SPOKEN OF a great deal in the Bible, but nothing is said in its praise. On the contrary, it is called "the house of bondage," because, for two hundred years the Israelites were slaves in the land.

The greatest honour that Egypt ever received was being visited by the Lord Jesus, when he was a little child. After His ascension into heaven, one of His disciples went to Egypt to praise the Gospel. A great many Egyptians became Christians in his days, but very few are Christians *now*.

It was the Arabs who made them change their religion. They came with their swords in the name of the false prophet Mahomet. Those who would not believe in Mahomet were forced to wear round their necks a very heavy cross, so heavy that the weight could hardly be borne. A few of the Egyptians refused to become Mahomedans, and their descendants still live in the land, and are called Copts.

❖ ❖ ❖ ❖ ❖

## THE RICH EGYPTIANS.

THE GREATEST PEOPLE IN THE LAND are Turks, and live after the Turkish manner, while the common people are Arabs. This is the way in which a rich man spends his day.

He begins it by prayers, not to the true God, but to the God of Mahomet. Then his slave presents him with a cup of coffee and a pipe. Afterwards he goes out to the bath, to the shops, or to visit his friends. At noon he dines with his family. When any one wishes to be very kind to a friend, he takes nice morsels in his fingers and puts them into his friend's mouth.

After dinner a cup of coffee and a pipe are again presented. The evening is spent either in talking and playing at chess at home, or in paying visits by the light of a lantern. Such is the useless life of an Egyptian grandee. The mind is never exerted by reading or writing, nor the body by any active employment or exercise.

The Egyptian ladies live in upper rooms with latticed windows. None but ladies or their nearest relations are allowed to visit them. But they are allowed to go out; only they always wear a loose black silk wrapper, and a thick white veil,—so thick that the face cannot be seen through it.

Great ladies generally do not walk, but ride upon asses.

A lady often lets her little child ride before her on the ass, but sometimes she bids a slave carry it. The child sits on the *shoulder* of the slave. It is curious that in Asia—children should be borne on the side, in America on the back, in Europe in the arms, while in Africa, as you see, they are borne on the shoulder. I do not mean to say that in *all* parts of Africa they are carried thus—but in *one* part they are.

In most countries mothers take delight in dressing their children fine—indeed too fine—thus making the little creatures vain and trifling; but in Egypt, mothers, shining in silks, are often accompanied by children in old and shabby clothes. The reason is, that Egyptian mothers are afraid of the "evil eye." They suppose that evil spirits are envious of their little ones, and ready to do them harm, and therefore they are afraid of decking their children gaily, lest they should provoke them.

Knowing nothing themselves, they bring up their children in ignorance. They amuse themselves also by embroidering handkerchiefs with elegant patterns, and by making sherbert from various sweet fruits and flowers; one sort they make from violets. They have no better occupations than these.

❖ ❖ ❖ ❖ ❖

## THE CHARACTER OF THE EGYPTIANS.

THE WORST QUALITY IN ANY CHARACTER is hypocrisy, and this is to be found in the Egyptian. In Egypt it is thought a credit to be religious, therefore every one tries to appear to be so. People seem to think that they may do any wicked action they please, if they only just say, "I beg forgiveness of God!" A man will speak without shame of the lies he has told, and then just add, "I beg forgiveness of God!" as if God was too merciful to punish his sins.

It is a rare thing in Egypt to speak the truth. There was an Egyptian, by trade a jeweller, who was a man of his word. His countrymen were so much surprised to find he spoke the truth constantly, that they gave him the name of "The Englishman."

Though the Egyptians care little for truth, they care much for *charity*. They show their charity by giving to beggars, especially to the blind.

The best part of the character of the Egyptians is "respect for the aged."

❖ ❖ ❖ ❖ ❖

## THE COPTS.

*THEY ARE THE CHRISTIANS* of Egypt. When the Arabs conquered Egypt, more than a thousand years ago, the natives became Mahomedans,—except a few, whose descendants are still Christians. It might be expected that these Copts would be very good, because they are Christians; but they are not better than the rest of the nation. Like the rest, they are *deceitful;* and in one respect they are *worse*, for they are addicted to drinking brandy.

❖ ❖ ❖ ❖ ❖

## THE WONDERS OF EGYPT.

*THE PYRAMIDS ARE GREAT PILES OF STONES.* There is one much larger than the rest. It is possible to climb to the top, for the stones of the sides are uneven, like steps; yet the steps are so high that Englishmen find it very hard to clamber up such stairs; but some Egyptians can jump from stone to stone like goats, and they help travellers to get up and to get down.

But do you not inquire what is the use of these Pyramids? For a long while people were perplexed about it. At length an opening was found in the side of one of the pyramids. Then narrow, slanting passages were discovered.

To what do the passages lead? To dark chambers. In the largest a stone chest was found; it had no lid, and it contained nothing but rubbish. What a disappointment to those who expected to find treasures, or at least, the bones of ancient kings!

◇   ◇   ◇   ◇   ◇

## CAIRO.

*THIS CITY WAS BUILT* by the Arabs, who conquered Egypt, and it shows that they did not know how to build a city, for such crooked and narrow streets are seldom seen.

The worst evil is the dust, which is amazing, because only five showers fall in the course of the year, and there are sandy deserts all around Egypt. The dust renders many people blind.

Inside the houses of Cairo there are multitudes of enormous spiders, buzzing flies, and biting mosquitoes. Nor are these the worst enemies; rats run boldly about the room, and snakes and scorpions creep slily in. Cairo *might* be a beautiful place, with its numerous gardens and magnificent mosques, but it *is* a most odious city. Lately, however, some fine wide streets have been built.

## *NUBIA.*

Egypt, under Turkish rule, conquered ancient Sudan between 1813 and 1822, establishing Khartoum as the territory's capital in 1821. The inhabitants were regarded in the mid-nineteenth century as strict Mohammedans who ate little meat and engaged in "primitive methods" of commerce, selling maize by the handful. Nubian exports included dates, ebony and ivory, ostrich feathers, coffee, cotton, rhinoceros and elephant hides, and gold dust.

THOSE WHO WISH TO VISIT NUBIA ought to go there in a boat, for there is no other pleasant way. The Nile in Nubia flows between high rocks of various forms, with waterfalls roaring like thunder amongst the little isles below, so that the scenery is grand. In some places it is lovely, and there are beautiful palm-trees, laden with dates, close to the water's edge.

But the most interesting objects are the ruins of the temples. These temples were built thousands of years ago, even before the Israelites were slaves in Egypt.

There are also ancient tombs in Nubia, and these also are hewn out of the rocks.

But what is Nubia now? A Mahomedan country. It has been conquered by Egypt, and it has followed the religion of Egypt; yet the people are so savage that they hardly know what religion they are.

*THEY ARE NOT A BRAVE NATION.*

One of their delights is to dance by moonlight around large fires, and as they dance, to play strange antics, and to make strange noises, acting more like demons than like men.

There are many miserable villages among the rocks. The huts are the loose stones, thatched with dry stalks. The men wear white calico caps (not *red*, like the Egyptians). Their garments are a shirt and trousers. They are a fine race of people, tall and strong, and of a dark copper colour; their eyes are large and bright, their faces broad and round, their noses and their lips rather thick.

# *ABYSSINIA.*

Some forty years before Italy conquered Eritrea (and nearly a century before it took Ethiopia), Abyssinia was the stomping ground of a procession of explorers. Dr. Charles Tilstone Beke arrived in 1840, followed by Mansfield Parkyns and Dr. J. L. Krapf in 1843. Later in the decade, Lij Kassa, warlord of the western district of Kujara, led a failed revolt against the ruling Turks, but after conquering the provinces of Godjam and Tigré, he named himself Emperor Theodore III, King of Ethiopia, in 1855. "Dead bodies are seen lying in the streets and serve as food to dogs and hyænas," warned the 1854 *Encyclopædia Americana.* "Marriage is . . . formed and dissolved at pleasure; conjugal fidelity is but little regarded . . . There is no country where the natives are of so many shades of colour; some are almost black, and others almost white. The people are a fine race, tall and strong; and even those who are black have good features."

*THE MEN NOT ONLY DELIGHT* in copper and silver rings, but they take pride in an ornament which leads them to commit dreadful wickedness. Their chief glory consists in a sprig of asparagus in the hair, because it is the token of having slain an enemy; every one, therefore, who has never killed one, is on the watch for an opportunity of slaughter, even if it be only of a helpless child.

The food they carve is *raw* meat. They never roast or boil, and they laugh at other nations for *burning* their meat. Twice a-day they sit down to their horrible repasts;—at noon, and again at sunset;—and they devour the flesh with the eagerness of wild beasts.

Yet these barbarous men, who delight in slaughter, attend to the dressing of their hair as much as the women, either dividing it into ringlets, or frizzing it in bunches, and always soaking it in rancid butter.

❖ ❖ ❖ ❖ ❖

## THE HABITATIONS OF THE PEOPLE.

*THE FLOORS ARE OF MUD,* and are freely trodden by mules and poultry. A chafing-dish is used to give warmth, and as there is no chimney, the walls are covered with soot. A fire is not needed for cooking, as cooking is despised. The beds are merely bullock-skins, in which the people wrap themselves at night, after having spent the evening in drinking many gallons of beer.

There is no neat garden in front, but only heaps of rubbish; and water is never used to clean either the dwelling or those who dwell in it.

RELIGION.—Perhaps there is no Christian country in the world as ignorant as Abyssinia. How should the *people* know anything, when the *priests* know nothing! Their chief employment is dancing and singing.

In general the Abyssinians avoid everything that the Mahomedans approve, for they hate and despise them, and wish to be as unlike them as possible. On this account they never smoke, nor drink coffee, nor wash frequently.

It would be well if they were like the Mahomedans in temperance, instead of giving themselves up to devouring raw flesh, and drinking beer to excess.

See that little round white hut, with a thatched and pointed roof thickly shaded by high trees. It is a church. Enter, but beware not to go too far in. The middle is so sacred that only the *chief* priest may approach, for there lies concealed the ark—which is the communion table. We see how these Christians have imitated the Temple of the Jews—and this is a great error—for the Jewish mode of worship ought not to be followed by us.

The morning service on Sundays begins at seven. The congregation, standing all round, gaze at the priests in the midst, drumming on their drums, tinkling with their timbrels brandishing their crutches, and accompanying their music with a loud howling. This noise is thought to be honourable to God. How different is it from the solemn prayers and hymns of the churches of England!

On Wednesday and Friday they eat nothing till evening, and then only boiled wheat, or pea, or cabbage soup. They might eat fish, but they cannot often get it, as there are so many waterfalls from the hills, that the fishes are frightened away from the streams. On the whole, more than *half the year* is spent on fasting.

But then, to make up for all this *fasting*, there are two days in every week for *feasting:* these are Saturday and Sunday. These days they think were made for feasting, and upon them they eat an enormous quantity.

As *two* days in every week are spent in fasting, and *two* in feasting, *three* only remain for working,—Monday, Tuesday, and Thursday.

**CHARACTER.**—The Abyssinians seem to be very little better than heathens or Mahomedans; yet they are better in one respect. They are more *ashamed* of their wickedness; they tell lies, but they are ashamed of them. Parents punish their children for stealing very severely. One mother, who loved her children very much, punished her little girl for stealing honey, by burning the skin off her hands and lips;—the hands that were thrust into the jar, and the lips that tasted the stolen sweets.

Children are trained up to behave well. The boys are sent to keep sheep upon the hills, and the girls are employed at home in fetching wood and water, and in grinding corn. It is only the children of rich people who are taught to read, and then—it is only the boys. They are taught to read the Scriptures, but as it is in a language they do not understand, they might as well not learn at all.

Fondness for eating is a common fault. The people eat most voraciously, taking as large mouthfuls, and making as much noise with their lips, as possible; for they say, "None but a slave eats quietly."

They are not a brave nation. The sight of a wild elephant fills a whole troop of men with terror; and an Englishman who was not afraid to shoot one was considered a wonder.

Yet they are very cruel; cruel—to *animals,* tearing limb from limb, and eating their bleeding flesh, while warm and quivering;—cruel to *men,* killing even the helpless children of their enemies, in order to gain the honour of a sprig of asparagus.

# SOUTH AFRICA.

In 1852, the United Kingdom recognized the South African Republic, following decades of chaotic social upheavals and bloody conflicts among the British, the Boer farmers of largely Dutch descent, and the indigenous Bantu and Zulu societies. The Boers, angered by the British Empire's 1833 abolition of slavery, resisted the colonialist yoke by fighting their way into Zulu territory, establishing a sovereignty in central South Africa's Orange River Valley and seizing Zulu-ruled lands in Natal in the southeast. Britain overpowered the Boers and the Bantu in Natal in 1843 and in the Orange Free Sovereignty in 1848 but recognized the Boers' independent Oranje Vrijstaat, the Orange Free State, in 1854. Dr. David Livingstone ("...I presume"), a Scottish agent of the London Missionary Society, "discovered" Botswana's Lake N'Gami in 1849 and Zimbabwe's Victoria Falls in 1855.

❖ ❖ ❖ ❖ ❖

## THE CAPE COLONY.

*HAVE YOU EVER REMARKED* the shape of Africa? Broad at the top, it ends in a point. The point is called the Cape of Good Hope. The name of Good Hope was given to it by the first sailors from Europe that had sailed by it; they were delighted they had got so far, and they felt a *good hope* of reaching India.

Afterwards sailors from Holland came to the Cape, and a great many Dutchmen settled in the land. These Dutchmen are called

"Boors." There are farms also belonging to Englishmen; for the Cape *now* belongs to England.

◇ ◇ ◇ ◇ ◇

## THE HOTTENTOTS.

*THE CAPE OF GOOD HOPE* was once inhabited only by Hottentots, a miserable race of people, often called, in contempt, "Totties." They are about five feet high, they have woolly hair, little twinkling eyes, flat noses, high cheekbones, thick pouting lips, and yellow skins. They are weak and thin, and have small hands and feet. Their language is very harsh, and has a click in it, made by striking the tongue against the roof of the mouth, and their speech sounds something like the gobbling of turkeys.

*Once* these Hottentots were a savage people; but *now* those living near the Cape are not savage. *Once* they were thickly covered with grease, and wrapped in sheep-skins, but *now* the men wear jackets and trowsers, and the women dress in gay-coloured cotton gowns, and twist a red handkerchief round their heads. They have even left off their clicking language, and speak Dutch or English in their broken manner. They have left off, also, their savage manners; they used to tear open a sheep with their hands, and suck its warm blood, like tigers; then cut up its flesh in strings, just heat them for a minute on the ashes, and then let them down their throats, as they would let down snakes.

But have they left off their wicked practices? They used to drink to excess, and they do so still; they used to delight in idleness, and they do so still; they used to tell lies, and they do so still.

Have not the Dutch boors, who have lived among them so long, taught them about God and his holy laws? Oh no; these boors have treated the Hottentots like beasts. They said they were *almost* beasts.

How can that be? If the Hottentots have souls, they are as precious in the sight of God as we are. However, the boors found these Hottentots were more *useful* than beasts, and they set them to watch over their sheep and their goats.

When the English came, a law was made to force the boors to set the Hottentots free. This law made the Boors very angry, and many of them went to live higher up in Africa, beyond the bounds of the colony, where they could do as they pleased.

✧ ✧ ✧ ✧ ✧

## CAPE TOWN.

*THIS IS THE CAPITAL* of the Cape colony. It was built by the Dutch, and there are still many Dutchmen living there, as well as Englishmen. There are also many Hottentots, but they no longer look like savages, and they are useful as servants.

✧ ✧ ✧ ✧ ✧

## THE BUSHMEN.

*THEY ARE HOTTENTOTS*, but the most miserable of the race. A Bushman lives like a wild animal among the bushes. He has no hut, and no cattle; he has only a few things, such as he can carry about with him.

When a family are travelling, the man holds in his hand a spear, and on his back his bow and arrows; his wife carries the baby, as well as an earthen pot for cooking, and some ragged skins for a bed, and some eggs full of water. These eggs are ostrich eggs, very large and hard; they are pierced with a little hole, which is stopped with grass. Thus they supply the place of bottles. They are carried in a net bag. The Bushmen show some cleverness in finding out such a way of carrying water and eggs. But they have no thought, except about getting food, and defending themselves from foes.

As they are great robbers, they have many enemies. Having no cattle of their own, they seize the cattle of the Hottentots, and of the Dutch boors whenever they can.

The Bushmen beat their children cruelly, and sometimes kill them in a rage. There is an instance reported, of a father who acted in a still more barbarous manner. A lion came at night to this Bushman's hole, and refused to go away without a supper; the unnatural father threw one of his little ones to the wild beast to satisfy its hunger, and make it go away.

The Bushmen's children are often stolen by the Hottentots, and sold to the boors as slaves. As these children are generally wandering far away from their parents, it is easy to steal them. The little Bushmen are more miserable with their Dutch masters than they are when roaming about their country, getting food as they can.

Though Bushmen are counted among the most stupid of men, yet they can do many things better than any other Hottentots. When they shoot their arrows, they seldom miss the mark. They can climb rocks so steep, that no human foot could follow them, and they can run very nearly as fast as a horse can gallop.

Have the Bushmen any God? None but an INSECT! It is a curious insect, about the size of a child's little finger, and it builds itself with straws a little house. SUCH IS THE BUSHMEN'S GOD! The greatest honour any one can receive, is for this god to light upon him; he is then reckoned a very happy man. The greatest sin any man can commit, is to kill one of these creatures. A young German, having caught one, told the Bushmen he was going to kill it. The foolish people threw themselves on the ground in agony, and with tears and cries entreated the stranger to let it go; and when it was set free, they jumped for joy.

✧ ✧ ✧ ✧ ✧

## THE CAFFRES.

*THESE PEOPLE LIVE VERY NEAR* the Hottentots, yet they are not at all like them, for they are tall, strong, and fine-looking men. They are not timid like the Hottentots, but bold and fierce. The Dutch boors have not been able to make slaves of *them*. Yet they are savage and ignorant.

The Caffres think a great deal of their appearance; but they wish to look terrible, rather than handsome. For this purpose they make their woolly hair stick out as much as possible, and they smear both their hair and their bodies with red paint.

The women do all the hard work. They plough,—they sow,—they reap,—they mow,—they build;—and the men do nothing when at home, except milk the cows; but they are often out hunting or fighting. These poor women are worse used than the oxen they tend. They are worse fed too, and are always thin and miserable,—stunted in their growth, and stooping in their figures.

Cruelty is the chief vice of the Caffre.

The Caffres tear out the inside of their enemies, and eat part of them. When they take women prisoners they are anxious to get their brass rings off their fingers, and, finding that they will not come off easily, they cut off the women's hands.

The most horrible of all their customs is *this;*—when a man becomes a chief he is washed first in blood! In what blood? In human blood! In whose blood? In the blood of his *nearest relation!*

It is a fearful thing to live in the midst of the Caffres. Many of the Dutch boors have been slaughtered, as well as some of the English settlers.

✧ ✧ ✧ ✧ ✧

## THE ZOOLUS.

*THEY ARE A TRIBE* of Caffres, and the fiercest of all. They are the darkest, for they live nearest the equator; some of them are almost black, but the usual complexion is dark chocolate.

They have a very strange way of dressing their heads. Instead of making their hair stick out, as other Caffres do, they cut it all off, except a little at the top of their heads. To this little hair which is left they fasten a ring made of rushes, which lies, like a kind of crown, flat upon the top of their heads. They *could* not, like the Chinese, grow their hair long; for their hair is woolly, and it will not grow long.

The chief dress of the men consists in strips of cats' fur, tied to a girdle round their waists. When they go to war, they wear cats' tails dangling to their girdles, a cap of otters' skin, and over their shoulders, as ornaments, the long hairs of ox-tails. In one hand they hold a shield, and in the other a spear. The shields are often made of the skins of white oxen, and they have a striking effect when held by hands nearly black.

❖ ❖ ❖ ❖ ❖

## THE BECHUANAS.

*THIS RACE OF MEN ARE,* like the Caffres, tall and strong, and of a very dark-brown colour; and they are *not* like the little yellow Hottentots. Like the Caffres, they are governed by chiefs, or little kings.

**MANNERS.**——The Bechuanas never bathe, but cover their bodies with mutton fat and red ochre. In this respect they differ from the Zoolus, who bathe every day. The Bechuanas were surprised when they first saw white men burn candles; they wondered at their wasting valuable grease in that manner, instead of smearing it on their bodies.

They always laugh when they hear of customs unlike their own;

*THEY NO LONGER LOOK LIKE SAVAGES,*
*AND THEY ARE USEFUL AS SERVANTS.*

for they think that they do everything in the best way, and that all other ways are foolish. The Bechuanas, however, are not quite as idle as the Caffres, for they undertake the labour of making the skin-cloaks, whereas the Caffres lay it all upon the women. The Zoolus wear no cloaks at all.

**CHARACTER.**——They commit dreadful crimes. Once, a man fell into a passion with his wife, and seizing his spear he killed her on the spot. But he was not ashamed of what he had done. Next day he was seen walking about quite unconcerned, while the hyenas were feasting upon his wife's dead body.

It may be supposed the Bechuanas think nothing of murdering their own little babies when convenient. They are so cruel as sometimes to bury them alive.

There are various tribes of Bechuanas. There is one tribe who are CANNIBALS. They were first induced to eat human flesh from having no cattle, and now they prefer it to any other food.

# WESTERN AFRICA.

---

## GUINEA,
### OR NEGROLAND.

In the 1840s and 1850s, European powers fought for trading territory in West Africa, but the region was increasingly settling under the rule of the English and the French, who proclaimed the coast a protectorate in 1849. Guinea's boundaries were still loosely defined in the 1850s, but as the epicenter of "the Slave Coast"—and a source of commerce abolished (at least officially) by the British in 1833—the region by mid-century was instead exporting indigo, sugar, pepper, and palm oil. Freed slaves lived in two West African colonies: British Sierra Leone, founded in 1787, and American Liberia, founded in 1822 and granted independence in 1847. By 1854, Guinea was still a mystery to the West; one encyclopedia noted, skeptically, that "even the problematical unicorn is said to exist in the interior."

*THE NEGROES ARE KNOWN* all over the world, as the unhappy people who have been made slaves by so many nations. The British people were *once* so wicked as to steal Negroes, and take them to distant lands to work as slaves till they died. But now these cruel practices are not allowed by our laws.

Negroes are often to be seen walking in the streets of London, but they are not *slaves*. They are quite black; with a flat nose, thick pouting lips, woolly hair, and teeth of dazzling whiteness.

The Negroes live in some of the hottest countries of the world.

Very near their country is the great desert of Sahara, and the air passing over that desert becomes so dry and burning, that it feels like a blast from a hot furnace.

Yet Negroland is more beautiful than Caffreland, because of the fine forests and broad streams.

Instead of dressing in *skins,* the Negroes wear *calico* garments, which are much cooler and cleaner, and which they weave from the cotton plant. The Caffres had no idea of a God till taught by Christians, but the Negroes have a great reverence for frightful images of clay, which they call their Fetish.

❖ ❖ ❖ ❖ ❖

## ANECDOTES OF NEGRO KINGS.

*THERE ARE A GREAT MANY KINGS* scattered over the land. Travellers who bring *presents* to these kings are generally well received, but travellers who do *not* are ill-treated.

These were the presents given on one occasion to the king of Boossa: a pair of silver bracelets, a looking-glass, and a tobacco-pipe. With these he was so much delighted, that he never took his eyes off them for half an hour. His queen then asked the travellers for a present, and they gave her some plated buttons. She was admiring them, when the king saw them and snatched them away. The queen tried to get them back, but after a long struggle the king succeeded in getting them all into his own hands: he then picked out the largest and brightest for himself, and let his wife have the remainder. Yet you must not suppose that this king was a bad husband, for he was one of the best in Africa; only he behaved as other Negroes do—like a naughty child in the nursery.

At a great feast in the open air he danced before his subjects, yet he was a large and heavy man, not at all fitted for dancing. In one of the dances he imitated the canter of a horse, and cantered into one of his own huts amidst the applause of the spectators.

This king was not always engaged in these foolish amusements. He was usually employed in making his own clothes, and in attending to this business of his household. Most of the African kings waste all their time in sleeping, smoking, and talking.

The Fetish images are worshipped in some Negro kingdoms.

Behold that frightful image of clay! It is placed in a shed, and it stands on a bar of wood, like a bird upon a perch. The priests declare that it enjoys the smell of roast beef, and therefore joints are cooked just beneath; and no doubt, if the image likes the *smell,* the priests like the *taste* of roast beef much better.

*BEHOLD THAT FRIGHTFUL IMAGE OF CLAY!*

# AS - HAN - TEE.

The nineteenth-century population of the interior of the Gold Coast, a largely British region of what is now Ghana, was estimated at one million to three million, with many Muslim inhabitants migrating from Senegal and Niger. The wars of the 1820s resulted in a British peace treaty in 1831, when the Ashanti king was forced to surrender six thousand ounces of gold and his son as a prisoner to the English coastal settlement of Cape Coast Castle. Denmark in 1849 ceded to England the settlements of Christiansburg and Friedensburg.

THIS IS ONE OF THE GREATEST KINGDOMS in Africa. There is no court more splendid than the court of the king of As-hantee. All around him glitters with GOLD. He wears strings of gold beads round his neck, arms, knees, and ankles, and gold rings upon his fingers. His throne is a stool covered with gold. His guards, like himself, shine with gold.

Over the heads of the king and his nobles immense umbrellas are held by slaves—so immense as to shade thirty persons at a time.

Each noble is attended by a band of musicians, playing on various loud instruments; some play on gong-gongs, and some on horns made of elephant tusks; but the most tremendous sounds are produced by the great drums.

It is the custom for each noble to have a tune of his own. It might be amusing to hear these different tunes, if *one* were played at a time, but that is not the case. All the tunes are played at once, and the confusion cannot be described.

They have their songsters, or poets, whose business it is to set forth their praises. Thus they make themselves like gods, though they are but men.

But we may rather say they are like devils, such is their dreadful cruelty. When a nobleman dies one of his slaves is always put to death, that he may have some one to wait upon him in the world whither he is going. When a *king* dies, a *hundred* slaves are slaughtered, as well as his wives.

These wicked deeds are the consequences of the wicked religion of As-han-tee. The people worship all manner of gods, such as rivers, rocks, and trees; but they have worse gods than these. In one place a CROCODILE was worshipped!

---

# *DAHOMEY.*

"The ferocity which prevails among the nation almost surpasses belief," noted a breathless 1854 encyclopedia entry on the still-unknown interior kingdom of Dahomey. "Human skulls form the favorite ornament in the construction of the palaces and temples." Between 1842 and 1853, King Gezo launched expansionist wars to control slave-producing regions but was halted by Abeokuta, a town in today's Nigeria, which was fortified with the latest in European weapons. The region that would become Benin and Nigeria, once a fruitful source of slaves for Brazil, Haiti, and America, diversified after slavery was largely repudiated in the nineteenth century with a thriving trade in palm oil, maize, millet, and Guinea corn. Dahomey's increasingly educated population began to chafe under colonial (and largely French) rule; the British destroyed Eko, or Lagos, in 1852, and proclaimed it a possession in 1861.

*THIS IS ANOTHER OF THE GREAT KINGDOMS* of Africa. In one respect it is worse than As-han-tee; for it is full, not only of cruel *men,* but of cruel *women.*

The king has an army of *women,* as well as one of men. He trains these women to fight, and rewards them for their bloodshed. The business in which he chiefly employs them is seizing slaves, that he may sell them and obtain large sums of money.

The king feels great confidence in this army, and sends them continually to surprise the villages of his enemies.

This cruel king renders all the neighbouring kingdoms wretched by his ravages. How horrible is the slave trade! But if the *heathen* who *capture* the slaves are guilty, how much more guilty are the *Christians* who *purchase* them!

*THAT MONARCH RESTS HIS ROYAL FEET UPON A FOOTSTOOL*
*ORNAMENTED WITH THE SKULLS OF THREE FALLEN KINGS;*
*HIS WALKING-STICK ALSO IS HEADED BY A SKULL;*
*AND HIS GRANDEST DRINKING-CUP IS A SKULL.*

# AMERICA.

---

NORTH AND SOUTH AMERICA are called by us the New World, because they were not known by our part of the world in old times.

America is never spoken of in the Bible.

Once only savages lived in America; now there are very few savages, and a great many civilized people.

Yet there is room for a great many more—for there are fewer people in America, in proportion to its size, than in any other quarter of the globe; but new people are going there from Europe every day, and are making new roads, ploughing new fields, and building new cities.

---

# THE UNITED STATES.

In 1848, the end of the Mexican-American War yielded an enormous swath of new western territories for a prepubescent United States to gulp up. A rapid succession of presidents—Zachary Taylor, then Millard Fillmore, then Franklin Pierce—oversaw a clear return on the wartime investment, as prospectors rushed to California with sifting pans. By 1854, the Gold Rush was largely over, and a rash of fires in the infant city of San Francisco and a cholera epidemic in Sacramento had already made pioneer life a bit of a chore. Back east, New York City was teeming; nearly six hundred thousand of its three million residents had arrived within the previous decade. The *Daily Times* (later, the *New York Times*) started rolling off the presses in 1850. Midwestern state universities opened their doors in Michigan in 1845, Wisconsin in 1848, and Minnesota in 1851. Harriet Tubman stole across the Mason-Dixon Line in 1849; the following year, the Fugitive Slave Act forbade the assistance of escapees. Square dances (and round dances) were in full swing. The number of libraries in the U.S. tripled between 1825 and 1850; as the liberal-minded thumbed through Harriet Beecher Stowe's *Uncle Tom's Cabin* and Henry David Thoreau's *Walden*, more bloodthirsty readers picked up Herman Melville's *Moby Dick*. P. T. Barnum was discovering a sucker born every minute.

THIS IS AN IMMENSE COUNTRY, full of white people, speaking the English language, yet not calling themselves English people, but Americans.

A long while ago a great many English people went over and settled in America, and at first they paid taxes to our government, but at last they refused to pay any more; and when an English army was sent to *make* them pay, they fought and conquered that army.

❖  ❖  ❖  ❖  ❖

## NEW YORK

*NEW YORK IS THE CHIEF CITY.* It contains about a quarter as many people as London. It is much more beautiful, for it has neither smoke nor fog, but enjoys a clear and brilliant sunshine. In warmth it is like Spain or Italy.

There is in New York a very broad street, called Broadway, planted with trees; it is two miles long. It is thronged with splendid carriages, and people elegantly dressed.

❖  ❖  ❖  ❖  ❖

## BOSTON.

*THIS CITY IS MORE TO THE NORTH* than New York, and therefore is not so hot; neither is it so rich, nor so gay. Yet, like New York, it is free from smoke and fog, and so the various objects have a bright appearance. But there is no splendour nor grandeur. There are very few carriages to be seen in the streets, nor elegant ladies displaying their dresses; but there are, instead, scholars of all ages hastening with their books to join their classes.

❖  ❖  ❖  ❖  ❖

## NEW ORLEANS.

*THIS IS THE GAYEST CITY* in America, and also the most ungodly. There are very few churches, but there are amusements of all kinds. It may be called a city of strangers, for people come from all parts of America to pass the winter here.

There is no place in the whole world where so many ships are all collected in one spot, as in the harbour of New Orleans. But the river is the bane of the city. The banks are so low that the damps from the water render the city unwholesome. Yellow fever frequently comes and carries away thousands. New Orleans is a dangerous place to live in, both for the body and the soul.

✧  ✧  ✧  ✧  ✧

## WASHINGTON.

*THIS IS THE GOVERNMENT CITY.* It cannot be called the *royal* city, because there is no *king* in the United States; but there is a President. He is the chief ruler, yet not all his life long. At the end of four years he goes out of office, and another President is chosen.

Washington is one of the most desolate cities in the world: not because she is in ruins, but for the opposite reason—because she is unfinished. There are places marked out where houses *ought* to be, but where no houses seem ever likely to be.

**CUSTOMS AND APPEARANCE.**——As the Americans are descended from the English, of course their customs are nearly alike. Yet there are points of difference.

The Americans do not drink as much ale and spirits as the English.

But there is one very unpleasant custom in America—it is chewing tobacco. Smoking tobacco is unpleasant, but less so than chewing it.

It might be supposed that the Americans would be just like the English in appearance, but they are not. Round and rosy cheeks, so common in England, are rare in America. Whenever a ruddy complexion is seen, a plump face, and a stout figure, the Americans guess that the person is from England. It is chiefly the heat of the climate which has made them so different from their English ancestors.

The children are brought up in a very unwholesome manner. At the dinner table of the boarding-house they see all kinds of dainties, and they are allowed to eat hot cakes and rich preserves at breakfast, and ices and oysters at supper, when they ought to be satisfied with their basin of porridge, or their milk and water and bread and butter. The consequence is that many children die, and others are pale and sickly.

*THE SPANISH CALIFORNIANS ARE A FINE RACE OF PEOPLE, BUT FOND ONLY OF AMUSEMENT.*

**SLAVES.**—There are about thirty States in America. Those in the north have better laws and customs than those in the south. In the Southern States SLAVERY prevails. The slaves are Negroes; most of the slaves now living were born in America, but their parents, or their grand-parents were stolen from Africa.

Some people declare, that these slaves are as happy as free labourers.

The slaves show plainly, that *they* do not think themselves happy, by often running away. Every day there are advertisements in the newspapers for runaway slaves. Just above each notice there is a little black figure of a Negro, running very fast, and carrying a small bundle at the end of a stick.

There are indeed kind masters, who do not allow their slaves to be ill-used. Slaves love such masters; but still they would rather not be slaves at all.

Masters are continually afraid lest their slaves should join together and rise up against them. They try to prevent themselves, by keeping their slaves in ignorance, that they may be stupid like the brutes, and not have sense to rebel. There is a law, forbidding any one to teach a slave to read.

But though the masters wish to keep the slaves in ignorance, they are ashamed of hindering them from learning the way of salvation.

Yet, even in church, the poor Negro is reminded that he is nothing but a slave; for he is not allowed to sit with the rest of the congregation. It is usual for the Negroes to be placed in a gallery, quite separate from the white people.

In some cities there are separate chapels for the blacks. White people may go to them if they please, but they seldom do. One traveller entered a chapel in Savannah (a city of the south), and he found himself to be the only white man there amongst six hundred blacks; even the preacher was a black. This black congregation were more earnest in their prayers than many white congregations are; they listened to the sermon with great attention, and sang the hymns with sweet accord.

It is no wonder if the poor creatures are lazy; they cannot earn wages, however hard they may work; they cannot lose their places, however little they may do. It is curious to see them in the sugar-cane fields, lifting up their hoes as slowly as ever they can.

How happy it would be if these slaves could be set free! A master may set a slave free when he pleases; but he may not allow him to remain in the Southern States, lest the other slaves should want to be free too. The free slaves are generally sent to the Northern States, where they are hired as servants.

There are no *slaves* in the Northern States, but there are many *blacks* there; and perhaps you think they are kindly treated as they are not slaves. Far from it. They are not beaten, it is true, but they are despised and insulted in every possible way. Is not this very wicked? Merely because they have a black skin.

The blacks may not ride in the same carriage on a railway, as the whites; so a separate carriage is always provided for them. No one will shake hands with them in the Northern States. In the Southern States it is common for masters and mistresses, when they are going on a journey, to shake hands with their black *slaves* at parting; but no such kindness is ever shown to black *servants* in the Northern States.

It is painful to see the manner in which many worthless whites behave to many harmless blacks. In New York, a big white boy, meeting a little black one, began to kick him. The poor child seemed used to such treatment, and ran away without saying a word.

**THE FORESTS.**——North America is a grand country. It is not yet filled with people,——nor is it yet deprived of its fine FORESTS. The railways pass through these vast forests. In going from one great city to another, instead of passing by fields of cattle and corn, as in England, travellers in America pass through forests for hundreds of miles, and only see now and then a log-hut, surrounded by a little patch of cultivated ground.

But the forests are not without inhabitants. Wild beasts are there, yet none so terrible as those in Africa and Asia.

There are, however, terrible snakes in the forests, especially the RATTLE-SNAKE. It is happy for men that it has a rattle. Some little bones rub against each other in its tail, as it moves along, and the noise warns men to flee away.

There are many harmless inhabitants of the forests. There are the PIGEONS. The foresters are glad at their arrival, for they knock them down and take them home to make into pies.

**THE PRAIRIES.**—No places can be more unlike than the forests and the prairies. There are no trees in the prairies; nothing but green grass sprinkled with flowers. Yet it is supposed, that once the prairies were forests, but that wandering savages set fire to them, and consumed them. Now they are desolate places.

There are some very curious animals called dogs, inhabiting the prairies. Yet, though *called* dogs, they are like dogs in nothing but in barking. (For while the *real* dogs of America do *not* bark, these do.)

**RELIGION.**—The government supports no ministers, but leaves the people to find ministers for themselves. In the great towns the people have provided themselves with many ministers; but there are large tracts of country without any.

**CHARACTER.**——There are so many slaves in the south, that the white people indulge in the habits of idleness and luxury. The children, from their earliest age, have black people ready to do everything for them; so they learn to do nothing for themselves. As they grow up, they leave all the work to the slaves, while they themselves lounge upon sofas, reading novels—or divert themselves with company.

The people in the Northern States are very industrious. As there are not many servants to be had, they wait upon themselves. The children are useful to their parents. They can be trusted to go on messages, and to make purchases, and even to go to the *dentist's* by themselves.

The Americans are benevolent. They love to do good, and among other things they have asylums for the blind, and hospitals for the sick, and refuges for the destitute; and they make even their *prisoners* comfortable—perhaps *too* comfortable.

# BRITISH AMERICA.

Britain's colonial North American borders with the United States were defined in the 1840s in Maine and along the 49th Parallel, extending to the Pacific Ocean. In 1848, Britain granted self-rule to the colonies of Nova Scotia, New Brunswick, and Upper Canada (Ontario) and Lower Canada (Quebec). In 1851, the most railroad track per capita in the world, 1,006 miles, connected the 1,840,000 inhabitants of Upper and Lower Canada; Newfoundland had no railroads—or roads, for that matter—but its 120,000 people were wired with four hundred miles of telegraph lines. The boomtown of Montreal was home to 57,716 people in 1852 and nearly 65,000 two years later. In 1846, Nova Scotia geologist Abraham Gesner invented a process for refining coal into kerosene.

PART OF AMERICA belongs to England; it is the northern part, and it is called British America. It consists of many countries.

The people of British America are our *fellow-subjects*, while those in the United States are *not*.

✧ ✧ ✧ ✧ ✧

## THE RIVER ST. LAWRENCE.

THIS RIVER DIVIDES British America from the United States. It is well that there *is* a river to divide them, for the people of these two countries do not agree well together. There is scarcely another river in the world to be compared to this river; not that it is so great a river, but it is so beautiful. It flows from the largest lake in the world (that is, the largest lake of *fresh* water), well called Lake Superior. This lake is so immense, that Ireland might be bathed in it, as a child is bathed in a tub; that is, if islands *could* be bathed.

**THE PEOPLE OF BRITISH AMERICA.**——There is a great difference between the manners of the people on the opposite sides of the river St. Lawrence.

On the British side they are more civil and respectful; on the other side—they are more industrious and temperate.

There are beggars on the British side; scarcely any on the other.

The people are given to drinking on the British side; they chew tobacco on the other side.

There is a great difference to be observed at dinner, in steam-boats and hotels. In the United States all is hurry and confusion; but in British America the people enjoy their meals in quiet and at leisure; for they have not so much business to do as the people in the United States, nor are they in such a hurry to grow rich.

In British America there are no slaves. There never can be any in countries that belong to Britain. Slaves of the United States, if they can escape to British America, are safe and free. Numbers therefore take refuge in this land. But it is very cold for black people.

❖  ❖  ❖  ❖  ❖

## NEWFOUNDLAND.

*THE NAME OF THIS LARGE ISLAND* makes us think of those dogs with which children can play,—they are so *gentle;* and on which children can ride,—they are so *large.*

In their native country they often save the lives of drowning men; for there are many ships wrecked on the coast of Newfoundland.

In no place are such dogs more wanted than in Newfoundland. Dead bodies are often cast upon the shore—sometimes as many as three hundred at once. Large chests are often washed by the waves on to the land. There are men called wreckers, who live by seizing all they can find; and they sometimes murder men who have escaped the waves, in order to get their clothes and money.

Newfoundland is a dreary abode. The summer indeed is pleasant, for there is abundance of green grass, and the herds of deer look beautiful feeding on the hills; but the winter is long and severe; the snow falls, and the winds howl, and the ships are wrecked upon the rocks.

❖   ❖   ❖   ❖   ❖

## THE NORTH AMERICAN INDIANS.

*ALL OVER AMERICA* there are wandering savages. Once there were a great many, now there are but few; and there are fewer and fewer every year, and so it is probable at last there will be none at all.

And why have they become so few? Because white men have come and taken possession of their lands—the grounds where they used to hunt, and the shores where they used to fish. They have perished also by the small-pox; and they have perished by the fiery waters—even rum and brandy.

The North American Indians are the finest race of savages in the world—the strongest, the bravest, the most generous and honourable. Yet they are very cruel. Their colour is singular: it is red, or rather copper colour.

These red men are divided into many tribes, each of which has a name, and usually a very strange one. There is the tribe of the Crows, and of the Crees,—the Blackfeet and the Flatheads, the Chipeways and the Ojibeways, besides many more.

These tribes differ from one another in their dress and their customs. The Crows are the finest of all the tribes. Some have hair ten feet long, and when they walk—it sweeps the ground like a train. Other tribes have tried to make their hair grow as long as the Crows, but have never succeeded. To make it *seem* as long, some Indians cunningly glue locks of hair to the end of their own hair; but the Crows look with great contempt on these pretenders.

It is the custom of some tribes for mothers to keep their babes in moss-bags, and never to take them out. When the mother travels she carries the moss-bag on her back.

If the babe dies while in his moss-bag (and no doubt many do), the mother places the dead babe in a tree, and keeps the moss-bag as a re-membrance. She stuffs it with black feathers, and often talks to the bag, as if the babe were still alive.

RELIGION.——The Indians do not worship idols. They believe there is a good Spirit, whom they call Father. But they believe also in an evil spirit, and they think that he is stronger than the good Spirit. Is not this idea enough to make them miserable?

They are always trying to defend themselves from the evil spirit. They have many foolish ways of doing so. Their chief trust is in their medicine-bag.

What is that? It contains neither rhubarb, nor senna, nor any kind

*ON THE BRITISH SIDE THEY ARE
MORE CIVIL AND RESPECTFUL.*

of medicine. By "medicine" the Indian means "mystery," or a secret charm.

When a boy is about fifteen he makes his medicine (for girls have no medicine-bags). He goes and wanders about the country, and when he comes back, he says he has had a dream about his medicine bag, telling him of *what* it is to be made. No one can know whether the boy is speaking truth or not. Whatever animal's skin the bag is to be made of, the boy must kill that animal *himself*, be it a great buffalo, or only a little puppy. Then he must keep his medicine-bag all his life long. If he lose his medicine-bag he is despised by all.

It is impossible to persuade an Indian to sell his medicine-bag; he values it more than his life. The Indian thinks thus with himself, "What would it profit me, if I were to gain the whole world and lose my medicine-bag?"

Every Indian has his medicine-bag (if he have not lost it), but every Indian is not a "MEDICINE-MAN." That is the highest honour an Indian can have. Every one who does anything that appears wonderful to the Indians, is counted a medicine-man.

One way of getting to be counted a medicine-man, is by making rain come; that is, by *pretending* to make it come.

When there has been no rain for a long while, the young men in the village assemble together. One of them undertakes to make the rain come; and he stands upon a high place, with a lance in his hand, pointing at the clouds, pretending to pierce them. The men try one after another; *one* is sure to get the title of medicine-man; for the rain is sure to come *at last*.

These medicine-men are the great deceivers of the Indians.

CHARACTER.——The most striking features in the character of the Indian are BRAVERY and CRUELTY. The children are encouraged to torment animals. The mother smiles to see her little ones tearing little birds to pieces.

The boys are early instructed in the art of taking scalps.

They are collected together in the open field, and are divided into two armies, each under the command of a man. They are taught to fight with blunt arrows. Every boy wears tuft of grass on his head, to represent a scalp. If an arrow strike him in a vital part, he is bound to fall down as *if* dead (though not at all hurt), and the boy who hit him runs towards him, and tears off the tuft of grass from his head, as *if* it were a scalp.

No wonder boys brought up in this way delight in fighting with *sharp* arrows when they are men.

# CALIFORNIA.

EVERY ONE HAS HEARD of California as a country abounding in gold. The inhabitants are descendants of Spaniards. There are only a few Indians left, and their number is lessening every day.

The Spanish Californians are a fine race of people, but fond only of amusement, especially of riding and gambling.

## ST. FRANCISCO.

THIS CITY IS AT THE MOUTH of the river Sacramento, and is the capital of California.

It is one of the most wicked cities in the world. Its grandest houses are gambling-houses. Sweet music is played within to attract the passers-by. If they enter, they see tables sparkling with piles of gold and silver, while anxious faces are passing cards from hand to hand.

Morning, noon, and night, the gambling continues, and gold that has been gained by a *year's* labour is lost in a few *minutes*.

Sometimes a man who has lost his all grows desperate, and struggles hard to keep his money. But he is soon silenced by one of the pistols hidden under the table. One day a lad was shot while gambling. The body was no sooner removed, than the murderer went on with his game, without fear of punishment.

Even on the Sabbath-day the gambling-houses are filled.

# GREENLAND.

Between 1847 and 1849, Denmark's thirteen colonies on the west coast of Greenland yielded £17,000 in imports of goods including fish, seal oil, reindeer skins, and eiderdown. Greenland's estimated 1851 population of ninety-four hundred included 250 Danes. "There seems to be no assignable limit to the capacity of an Esquimaux stomach," marveled an 1850s *Encyclopædia Britannica* entry. "He has been known to devour, in twenty-four hours, ten pounds four ounces of solid food, more than a pint of strong soup, and a gallon and a pint of water."

THIS NAME WOULD GIVE the idea of a land abounding in *green* trees and *green* grass. But Greenland is a land of snow and ice.

Snowland would be the right name for this country, and it was its *first* name. It was a deceitful man who gave it the name of Greenland, to persuade the people of Iceland to settle there.

HABITATIONS.——The Greenlanders use every method to keep themselves warm; yet very hard they find it to avoid being frozen in their beds. Several families live in one house, and the rooms are divided like stalls in a stable; each family have a stall, where they sleep at night and sit in the day.

A narrow wooden passage leads into the house; and it is so low, that it is necessary to creep along. No door closes the entrance, because if there were there would be no air in the house, and the inhabitants would be suffocated. As it is, the house is very close and unpleasant. The Greenlander uses water to drink, and to boil his food in, but not to wash himself, or his clothes.

FOOD.—There is no BREAD; for corn will not grow. There is a little fruit—crowberries, bilberries, and cranberries, and they are thought as much of as plums and cherries are here, and made into jam, not with *sugar*,—but with *oil*. The only vegetables are greens, and lettuces, radishes, and turnips.

There is no milk, nor butter, nor cheese, for the Greenlander has no *tame* reindeer to give him milk; all the reindeer are *wild*.

There is nothing for the poor Greenlander but fish, and the flesh of seals, bears, and reindeer, a few berries, and a few greens, with oil for sauce, and water to drink.

Do you feel inclined to pity the poor Greenlanders? Their summer so short,—their winter so long,—never cheered by the sight of green fields in spring,—nor of fruitful trees in summer,—nor of a golden harvest in autumn,—nor of a blazing hearth in winter.

Yet the Greenlander has his pleasures. During winter nights, the moon shines bright upon the snow, and there is a glorious light in the sky, called the Aurora Borealis.

In summer it is pleasant to rove from place to place. And their long summer nights, when the sun never sets, are sweeter than our summer days.

The Greenlander considered no country is to be compared with his; and he pines away when taken to another.

# THE WEST INDIES.

Jamaica, Britain's most prized Caribbean possession, was discovering the great economic costs of civil liberties. The 1838 abolition of slavery freed the vast black population—by 1853, 16 black legislators were serving in Parliament—but sparked the collapse of the island plantations' coffee, sugar and rum industries. The Dominican Republic broke from Haiti's two-decade rule in 1844 but accepted a return to Spain's colonization in 1861 in return for assistance in fighting Haiti. Spanish-controlled Cuba's riches in maize, rice, sugar, tobacco, cotton, timber and other resources were coveted by the Americans, the English and the French. In 1851, Spanish-American General Narciso Lopez led a failed revolt in Havana; five days after Spain executed 51 conspiring American liberators in mid-August, an angry mob in New Orleans sacked the Spanish consulate.

BETWEEN NORTH AND SOUTH AMERICA there lies a cluster of little islands, called the West Indies.

Most of them are very small indeed; but there are four of considerable size.

*Cuba* is much the largest of the islands. It belongs to Spain.

*Hayti* is the second in size. It did belong to Spain, but it has become free.

*Jamaica* is the third in size, and belongs to England.

*Porto Rico* is the fourth in size, and belongs to Spain.

In the islands of Cuba and Porto Rico there are numbers of Negro slaves, because these islands belong to Spain.

In Hayti the Negroes have made themselves free.

In Jamaica they have been set free by England.

❖ ❖ ❖ ❖ ❖

## JAMAICA.

*THOUGH ONLY* THIRD *IN SIZE*, this island is the *first* in beauty of all the islands of the Western Sea. There are not many islands in the world so beautiful, so fragrant, and so fruitful.

There are two plants which were *not* found in Jamaica when first discovered, which are now abundant. The tall sugar-cane grows in the sultry valleys—and the coffee-plant, with its dark green leaves and white blossoms, covers the sides of the hills.

The Spaniards discovered Jamaica—they killed all the poor Indians, and then brought Negroes from Africa. The English took the island from the Spaniards, and followed all their wicked ways.

These white masters tried to persuade themselves that the Negroes were little better than beasts.

At one time a law was made by the ungodly masters to forbid black people going into a church or chapel.

But this wicked law was changed by our good old king, George III, and the poor blacks crowded again into the churches and chapels.

And *now* there are no slaves in Jamaica! The Negroes are all free men!

It was a glorious day when they were made free. It was on the first of August, 1838.

Yet the *very next day*,—many blacks went to work as usual; only now they worked for wages, as free labourers.

However, it must be owned that there were other blacks, who became very idle now they were free. This is not to be wondered at. It is easy to get food in such a fruitful country as Jamaica, and it is natural in a hot country to dislike hard labour.

The industrious blacks live in great comfort.

The Negroes delight in giving names to their cottages. One is called Comfort Castle;—another—Canaan. Others are called Paradise, Freedom, Come See, A little of my Own, Thank God to See It. One has the singular name of—Me no Tinkee. What can that mean? It means, "Once I never thought I should have such a cottage, or, indeed, any cottage of my own at all."

The Negresses are too fond of dressing themselves fine, especially on Sundays. They like to be seen in white muslin gowns, with gay ribbons and green parasols. Even the men are fond of dress, and try to look like gentlemen. Once they could not wear clothes like Buckra (that is *white men*), but now they can if they please.

Many wear shirts and black hats, without being proud of them; but if a working Negro buys them in order that he may look like a gentleman, *then* he is proud.

There are very few white people in Jamaica now. Most are either black or brown.

# MEXICO.

The young republic, still reeling from its prolonged rebellion and breakaway from Spain, staggered through the 1830s and 1840s under the bellicose dictatorship of General Antonio Lopez de Santa Anna. Despite Mexico's recognition in 1845 of Texas's independence (and Texas's joining the United States), continuing border disputes sparked a three-year war with the United States in 1846. Mexico ceded much of what would become America's Southwest, from Texas to California, in May 1848. Santa Anna seized power again in 1852 and rekindled civil war until he fled the chaotic country in 1855. U.S. soldiers F. Maynard and G. Reynolds are said to have climbed Pico de Orizaba, Mexico's tallest mountain, in May 1848.

*THIS COUNTRY WAS ONCE CONSIDERED* the richest in the world. Every one spoke of the gold of Mexico. But *now* there is very little gold to be found there. California and Australia are the golden lines. There are, however, many *silver* mines in Mexico.

The capital of Mexico is Mexico.

Before the traveller reaches the city, he passes through the Black Forest. It is an awful place; not on account of wild beasts, but on account of wicked men who haunt it. By the road-side stand many crosses, to mark the spots where travellers have been murdered. It is pleasant to get out of this forest, and to find one's self among the hills. At last a beautiful valley is seen, with two smooth lakes, like silver mirrors glittering in the sun. There lies the great city of Mexico. No black cloud of smoke hovers over that fair city; for instead of being disfigured by chimneys, the flat roofs are adorned with blooming arbours. The traveller looks down upon the scene with enchanted eyes—then descends into the valley, to enter the city.

In most countries robbers are afraid of robbing at the gate of a city in the light of day; but in Mexico they escape punishment so often, that they grow very bold and daring.

Though Mexico is so beautiful at a distance, yet the streets are narrow and loathsome, and the poor people, walking in them, look like bundles of old rags.

There is a handsome square in the midst, where stand the fine cathedral and the palace of the President (for there is no king). Yet this square is crowded by noisy beggars called "Leperos." They stand in rows. Some, who have no legs, are mounted on the backs of their fellows, and they call out in a loud voice, "For the sake of the Most Holy Mother, bestow a trifle." If they get nothing, they begin to curse in an awful manner.

The churches of Mexico are very magnificent, with gold and silver altars, and gold and silver rails, and gold and silver cups. They contain many images superbly dressed.

In one church there was an image of the Virgin Mary arrayed in a blue satin robe, adorned with lustrous pearls. The priest often handed it to the worshippers on the floor to be kissed. Once a wicked lepero, when it was his turn to kiss it, secretly bit off one of the precious pearls, and carried it away in his mouth, without the theft being discovered.

But there are not many Mexicans as profane as this lepero, for even robbers respect the churches.

The poor people of Mexico cannot bear working, and they bring up their children in idleness.

Amongst the ragged people in Mexico may be seen the poor water-carrier, with jars of water in his hands, and as he goes along, he may be heard boasting of the sweetness and coolness of his burden.

It would be well if the Mexicans bought *more* of him, and *less* of those who sold the intoxicating liquor, "Pulque." It is a bitter beverage that no one likes at first, but it soon becomes a great favourite.

**ROBBERS.**——Mexico is indeed the land of robbers. They abound most in the country, because they succeed best there. It would be delightful to live in the country in Mexico, if it were not for the robbers.

In Mexico it is not thought a disgrace to be a robber. Even gentlemen, if they lose much money by gambling, will go and turn robbers for a little while, and not be ashamed.

Sometimes, however, a robber is caught and hanged, and his dead body suspended in chains by the road-side. But then he is much pitied.

The most honest set of people in Mexico are the letter-carriers. These men are employed in carrying packages as well as letters, and none but trusty men could obtain employment. What dangers must these carriers encounter from the robbers!

Robbers do not often break into the churches, but in times of tumult and rebellion they have even robbed churches.

❖　❖　❖　❖　❖

## THE INDIANS.

*THERE ARE MANY* of the Indians still living in the wild parts of Mexico, and a few near the towns. They are not slaves, but are as ill-treated as if they were. They are made to work in the silver mines, and are beaten by their overseers. Great pains are taken to prevent the poor creatures stealing the silver. People are appointed to watch them continually. But it is thought impossible that they should steal silver from the *furnace,* for *there* it is mixed with quicksilver, the fumes of which kill instantly.

There are poor Indians who live by catching poisonous spiders, for which they obtain three-halfpence each as a reward; but sometimes they die themselves of the bites.

# CENTRAL AMERICA.

---

THIS IS THE LAND THAT JOINS North and South America. Many have wished there was no such land, for it prevents our ships passing this way to China, though far the shortest way. Plans are made for making a canal and a railway across.

The Mosquito country is filled with black men, and the king is black. It is a heathen country.

---

# SOUTH AMERICA.

---

## BRAZIL.

In 1840, Brazil was an eighteen-year-old nation with a fourteen-year-old emperor, Don Pedro II, who oversaw a decade of new railroads, telegraph lines, banks—and war. A hostile British navy monitored and intercepted slave ships violating Brazil's 1826 abolitionist treaty; the public increasingly discouraged the illegal shipments of African labor, and the trade was stamped out in 1854 (although slavery itself was not). In 1849, Brazil suffered a yellow fever outbreak and a war waged by Argentine dictator Juan Manuel de Rosas, whose troops were crushed at Montevideo. The mid-nineteenth century boasted an enormous Brazilian caffeine buzz: coffee exports of £240,000 a year in 1818 would explode to more than £13 million by the early 1870s.

THIS IMMENSE COUNTRY is the daughter of that small country called Portugal. Thus Mexico is the daughter of Spain; and the United States are the daughter of England. All these have been rebellious daughters, and have refused to obey their mothers.

But Brazil, though she does not belong to Portugal, is governed by an Emperor.

There are very few people in Brazil, considering how large it is. There are not so many as in Ireland, that small island. Of these people very few are white. Some are dark people, called mulattoes, and some are Negroes.

❖ ❖ ❖ ❖ ❖

## RIO JANEIRO.

*THIS IS THE CAPITAL* of Brazil, and the largest city in all South America. Rio means river, and the city is often called only "Rio." There is not a city in the world in a more beautiful situation; it is close to the sea, yet embowered in green and flowery hills. The streets are so steep that Negroes carry up the great packages on their heads. They run all in a line, singing as they go.

❖ ❖ ❖ ❖ ❖

## THE RIVER AMAZON.

*THIS RIVER FLOWS THROUGH BRAZIL.* It is the LARGEST in the world. It is nearly two thousand miles long; it is one hundred and eighty miles wide at the mouth; in some places it is more than one hundred and twenty feet deep.

There are vast plantations of cacao-trees close by the Amazon. There are rich Portuguese gentlemen, who own these plantations, and who live in elegant villas by the river side. They lead very idle lives, for they need only exert themselves once a year when the fruit is ripe.

**RELIGION.**——The Roman Catholic religion prevails. Once a-year at Rio there is a grand procession of idols. The images are placed on stands, (like great trays,) and borne on men's shoulders.

Yet the people in Brazil are not so wicked as those in Mexico. One reason may be, there are not so many priests. The government pays the priests, and allows them so little money that few boys like to become priests.

People in Brazil do not sleep on beds on the floor, but in beds slung across the corners of the rooms. Four can be placed in one room.

*THE PEOPLE IN BRAZIL ARE NOT
SO WICKED AS THOSE IN MEXICO.*

These hammocks have two advantages; they are very cool, and they keep people out of the way of the reptiles. Idle people waste many hours of the day in their hammocks. A traveller was surprised in calling at a country house, at eleven o'clock, to find the lady swinging in her hammock, playing at cards with her husband, who sat in a chair beside her.

## PERU.

The Peruvian economy in the mid-nineteenth century went, very literally, to shit. Europe's demand for Peruvian guano demanded a mass immigration of Chinese laborers to replace the free workforce that disappeared in 1854, when slavery was abolished. Peru began exporting

guano in 1841; two decades later, an estimated 9.5 million tons had yet
to be mined. The twenty-four years following Peru's 1821 declaration
of independence from Spain were beset by war and revolution, but
Don Ramon Castilla's election to the presidency in 1845 instilled relative peace and prosperity. General Rufino José Echenique was elected
in 1851, but Castilla succeeded him for a second term four years later.
In 1846, thirty-foot idols adorned with silver were excavated from the
ruins of Tia-Huauacu, on the shores of Lake Titicaca.

*THIS COUNTRY IS AS FAMOUS* as Mexico for its gold and silver mines.

Peru resembles Mexico in many respects. Like Mexico, Peru belonged to Spain, and has rebelled, and has become a republic.

Like Mexico, Peru has the Roman Catholic religion.

Like Mexico, Peru has oppressed the Indians.

Like Mexico, Peru has set the Negro slaves free.

Like Mexico, Peru is full of gamblers and robbers.

*THE PEOPLE ARE CONTINUALLY EXPOSED*
*TO SUDDEN DEATH FROM EARTHQUAKES.*

Yet the *land* of Peru is not like the *land* of Mexico.

Peru consists of low sandy plains by the seashore, and of barren, bleak hills.

On those low sandy plains travellers have often perished from thirst, as sometimes there is not a fountain for thirty miles to-gether;—not a tree to give shade, nor a green bank where to rest. The bones of beasts which have dropped down exhausted are scattered along the way.

Many travellers, too, have perished in climbing the steep paths that lead to the high lands. Once a little family were on a journey; they had a mule; the father sat on it with the youngest child before him, and a boy of ten years old behind. As they went along, a huge mass of rock suddenly fell from the mountainside upon the head of the elder child, and hurled him into the river rolling beneath.

❖   ❖   ❖   ❖   ❖

## LIMA.

*THIS IS THE CAPITAL OF PERU.*

It is built on a low sandy plain, six miles from the sea.

Its inhabitants are in character like those of Mexico.

Even the ladies delight in bull-fights. The place for cock-fights is the finest in all the world. Robbers prowl near the city gates, and are seldom punished. Gambling is the amusement of all classes.

Yet the people are continually exposed to sudden death from earthquakes. Lima may be called "the city of earthquakes." Six times the city has been almost destroyed. About forty times in a year, the earth rocks and groans. Immediately,—though it be midnight, the people rush out of their houses, crying aloud, "Mercy!" The priests cause the bells of the churches to toll every ten minutes, and all the people hasten to prayers.

But after the rocking is over, both priests and people go on in their sins and their follies the same as ever before.

---

# *LA PLATA,*
## OR, THE ARGENTINE REPUBLIC

The seventeen-year dictatorship of Juan Manuel de Rosas, beginning in 1835, pitted his supporters—the conservative, livestock-herding Federalists in the lawless rural provinces, who demanded Argentine self-rule—against the urban Unitarians, who favored the central authority of Buenos Aires, the onetime capital of Bolivia, Paraguay, and Banda Oriental (later Uruguay). Rosas was overthrown in 1852, and the following year, Buenos Aires rejected Argentina's new constitution; its secession created two independent states that would be unified a decade later, after Buenos Aires defeated and absorbed the rest of Argentina. Livestock was Argentina's chief industry: the country was roamed by countless horses and cattle.

THIS COUNTRY, LIKE PERU AND CHILI, once belonged to Spain, and has rebelled, and become a republic. Yet the scenery and climate are quite unlike those of Peru and Chili.

La Plata consists chiefly of a vast plain, called the Pampas.

But are there no human inhabitants of this vast plain?

Yes, there are two sorts,—wild Indians; and—wild Spaniards, called Gauchas.

These Gauchas are not as wild as Indians; but they are as idle, and almost as ignorant. They live entirely upon beef; that is, upon the flesh of the wild cattle which they catch by means of the wild horses. They think it too much trouble to cultivate the ground, or even to keep cows. The Caffres in Africa have milk as well as beef; but the Gauchas are content with beef alone.

A Gaucha's hut is made of mud, and thatched with grass; the seats are HORSES' HEADS, and the cradle is a bullock's skin, fastened to the roof.

The fear of the Gaucha is, lest the Indians should come in the night, and burn his hut, and murder his family. As soon as he hears the wild shrieks of his enemies, he mounts a horse and tries to escape, but often *cannot*,—because the Indians can ride even more swiftly than he.

The *first* Spaniards who came to America murdered the Indians; and now the Indians murder these *last* Spaniards.

# THE GREAT
# PACIFIC OCEAN.

————•••————

THIS IS THE LARGEST OCEAN IN THE WORLD. There is no piece of *land* nearly as large as this piece of *water*.

It is studded all over with islands, called the "South Sea Islands." Some lie in clusters, and some quite alone in the midst of the mighty waters.

The largest of these clusters is New Zealand; for, though there are but three islands in this cluster, these three contain as much land as Great Britain herself (*not* including Ireland).

————•••————

# NEW ZEALAND.

The Pacific nation became a British colony in 1839, when traders began establishing settlements throughout the islands (Wellington in 1840, Christchurch a decade later). In 1843, the settlers' poorly translated, hotly disputed Treaty of Waitangi permitted British rule over the indigenous Maoris while allowing them full possession of the lands and forests. But the Maoris' eventual cooling to the treaty sparked bloody warfare until late 1847, when Britain established legislative and administrative powers. The governor, Sir George Grey, opened the legislative council a year later. The 1851 yield of 29,140 acres of wheat, barley, oats and potatoes boomed to 226,500 acres over the next decade.

THIS COUNTRY IS REMARKABLE for lying just *opposite* Great Britain. Could a tunnel be dug quite straight through the earth from our land, that tunnel would end in New Zealand. Such a tunnel, however, never can be dug. It would be eight thousand miles deep.

But men cannot dig so deep.

But though we can never reach New Zealand by a tunnel, yet we know that it lies just opposite to us, so that the feet of the people there are opposite to our feet.

All the SEASONS *there* are contrary to ours *here;* when it is summer there, it is winter here: and when it is winter there, it is summer here.

The seasons there are *like* ours here, though they occur at different *times;* and the days there are of the *same* length as the days here, though *they* also occur at different times.

It is remarkable also, that as our kingdom consists of two large islands, so New Zealand consists of two large islands. There is, indeed, a third, but it is so much smaller than the other two, that it is scarcely worth speaking of.

Which of the two islands should you suppose to be the colder? The northern island? Oh no. It is the hotter. In our land the north wind is cold, but in New Zealand it is warm; and the south wind is cold.

❖ ❖ ❖ ❖ ❖

## THE NORTHERN ISLAND.

*IN THE MIDST OF NORTH ISLAND* there are mountains *three* times as high as any in Great Britain, for some are ten thousand feet in height.

But there are *fires* amidst the snows, for some of the mountains are Volcanos. Terrible pits, deeper than the eye can pierce—scalding pools—nauseous vapours—and rumbling noises, are seen and heard,—felt and smelt—in that wonderful part of the island.

It is dangerous to walk among the boiling springs, for the ground is like a thin crust, which often cracks, and gives way. Yet these springs are useful in boiling food. A little girl, holding her baby sister in her arms, went one day to fetch a basket that had been placed in one of these holes: as she was passing along the narrow path, the babe fell out of her arms into the scalding water; the sister, anxious to save the babe, jumped in too, and quickly perished.

Who are the people inhabiting New Zealand?

They *were*, like their land, dangerous. They delighted in shedding blood, and even in *drinking* blood. They were warriors, and cannibals.

Such were the New Zealanders. But they are not such now.

A number of people used to live together in a "pa." A pa is a place enclosed by a strong wooden fence, and filled with huts. These huts were crowded together, and surrounded by all kinds of litter and rubbish. All day long the pa was a scene of confusion. The men sat in groups, talking loud, while they carved their spears, or mended their canoes, and they talked far more than they worked. The little children were running about; and the old men, rolled up in mats, were leaning idly against the walls of their huts. There was no neatness,— no quiet,—no comfort in the pa.

The appearance of these people was frightful and horrible. Their hair was one mass of oil and red paint, and their faces were cut about with a multitude of lines. This cutting was called "tattooing," and was considered ornamental, though really most disfiguring.

How different is a Christian village from a heathen pa!

There are *now* many clusters of cottages in New Zealand, with gardens neatly fenced, and carefully weeded, containing melons and pumpkins, potatoes, and kumera, and adorned with roses, and other lovely flowers. Kumera is a root of a sweet taste, and resembling a potato.

And there are CHURCHES now thronged with natives, decently clad, heartily uniting in the response, "Good Lord, deliver us!"—singing with sweet accord in their own tongue,—

"Praise God, from whom all blessings flow";

listening with breathless attention to the preacher's voice, declaring,—

"Behold the Lamb of God which taketh away the sin of the world."

Yet more missionaries ought quickly to be sent. For Roman Catholic priests are hastening to New Zealand; they have already persuaded many to believe in their vain words, and have even taught them to worship images, which New Zealanders, in their heathen state, never worshipped. The people are longing for missionaries. *Before* the missionary comes they build his house, and when he arrives, they receive him as an angel of God; but if the *priest* comes first, they will receive *him,* and learn to trust in things that cannot save.

❖   ❖   ❖   ❖   ❖

# HEARTFELT THANKS.

**PERSPIRATION.**——Peter Brooks and Jeremy Johnson at the Sheringham Museum, Sheringham, Norfolk. Neil Clarke at the Broseley Historical Society, Broseley, Shropshire. Saul Cohen at Sutin, Thayer, Brown, Santa Fe, New Mexico. Jennifer Owings Dewey. Colin Dickerman, Panio Gianopoulos, and all at Bloomsbury USA. Martin Fox. John Hodgman. Jeff Kastner and Sina Najafi at *Cabinet*. Meena Khorana at Morgan State University, Baltimore, Maryland. Carol Loomis at *Fortune*. Catherine MacKenzie at Christian Focus Publishing, Fearn, Ross Shire, Scotland. Paul Maliszewski and *The Denver Quarterly*. Gerry Mamaril. P.J. Mark and all at the Collins-McCormick Agency. Frank Martinez. Frederick Rankin McFadden, Jr. The New York Public Library: Humanities and Social Sciences Library, Rooms 100, 108, and 315, and the Schomburg Center for Research in Black Culture. Sam Potts. Adam Rowe and John Rowe. Scott Seeley and Ted Thompson at 826NYC, Brooklyn, New York. Stephanie Skirvin. Deborah Wassertzug. Pat Whalen. Patricia Wilson at the Time Inc. Archives, New York, New York.

**INSPIRATION.**——Heather Abel. Jason Adams. Tracy Bohan. The Book Den East, Vineyard Haven, Massachusetts. Dennis Cass. Emily Chenoweth and Jon Raymond. Paul Collins. John J. Edwards III and Becky Lowell Edwards. Dave Eggers and Vendela Vida. Nadine Ekrek. Dan Ferrara. Jennifer Gilmore. Joe Hagan and Samantha Hunt. Adam Hirschfelder. Farrin Jacobs. Joshua Kantro. Tave and Lynn Kaufman, Ina and Ira Pruzan, and all my cousins. Joyce Rutter Kaye. Aparna Mohan. Peggy Pfeiffer. Neal Pollack and Regina Allen. Marny Requa. Jennifer Sainato. Joanna Schaenman and Rob Sondik. Tina Shih and Gordon Strause. Yo La Tengo, "My Little Corner of the World." Jason Zengerle and Claire Farel.

**AND, OF COURSE.**——Rachel, and plenty of other Arturis. Jeff. Tracy. Mom and Dad.

**BOOKS, MOSTLY.**——Brooks, Peter: *Sheringham: The Story of a Town* (CROMER, ENGLAND: Poppyland Publishing, 2002). *Chambers's Encyclopædia: A Dictionary of Universal Knowledge for the People* (PHILADELPHIA: J. B. Lippincott & Co.; EDINBURGH: W. & R. Chambers. 1861–1865). Cutt, Margaret Nancy: *Ministering Angels: A Study of Nineteenth Century Evangelical Writing for Children* (BROXBOURNE, ENGLAND: Five Owls Press, 1979). Demers, Patricia, and Gordon Moyles: *From Instruction to Delight: An Anthology of Children's Literature to 1850* (TORONTO: Oxford University Press, 1982). *Encyclopædia Americana*, Ninth Edition (PHILADELPHIA: Maxwell Somerville, 1891). Haydn, Joseph: *Dictionary of Dates, and Universal Reference* (LONDON: Edward Moxon, 1853). Lieber, Francis, editor, assisted by E. Wigglesworth: *Encyclopædia Americana*, New Edition (BOSTON: B. B. Mussey & Co., 1854). Meyer, Louisa: *The Author of the Peep of Day: Being the Life Story of Mrs Mortimer* (LONDON: Religious Tract Society, 1901). Mortimer, Favell Lee: *The Countries of Europe Described* (NEW YORK: George Appleby & Sons, 1852); *Far Off: Asia and Australia Described* (LONDON: Hatchard & Co., 1852); *Far Off, Part II: Africa and America Described* (LONDON: Hatchard & Co., 1854). Ross, John M., L.L.D., editor: *The Globe Encyclopedia of Universal Information* (BOSTON: Estes & Lauriat, 1879). Urdang, Laurence, editor in chief: *The World Almanac Dictionary of Dates* (NEW YORK AND LONDON: Longman, 1982). Vincent, Benjamin: *Haydn's Dictionary of Dates Relating to All Ages and Nations: for Universal Reference* (NEW YORK: G. P. Putnam & Son, 1867). World Book Multimedia Encyclopedia V. 7.0, 2003.